The Basques by Jacques Allières

Series Editors
William A. Douglass, Gregorio Monreal, and Pello Salaburu

The Basques

Jacques Allières

Translated by Aritz Branton

With an introduction by Beñat Oyharçabal

Basque Classics Series, no. 11

Center for Basque Studies
University of Nevada, Reno

This book was published with generous financial support obtained by the Association of Friends of the Center for Basque Studies from the Provincial Government of Bizkaia.

Basque Classics Series, No. 11
Series Editors: William A. Douglass, Gregorio Monreal, and Pello Salaburu

Center for Basque Studies
University of Nevada, Reno
Reno, Nevada 89557
http://basque.unr.edu

Cover and series design © 2016 by Jose Luis Agote
Cover painting: "Pasajes de San Juan" by Juan de Echevarría

Library of Congress Cataloging-in-Publication Data

Names: Allières, Jacques, author. | Branton, Aritz, translator.
Title: The Basques / Jacques Allières ; translated by Aritz Branton ; with an introduction by Joaquín Gorrochategui.
Other titles: Basques. English
Description: Reno : Center for Basque Studies, University of Nevada, [2016] |
    Series: Basque classics series ; no. 11 | Includes bibliographical references and index.
Identifiers: LCCN 2016017872| ISBN 9781935709343 (hardback : alk. paper) |
    ISBN 9781935709435 (pbk. : alk. paper)
Subjects: LCSH: País Vasco (Spain) | Basques.
Classification: LCC DP302.B46 A4313 2016 | DDC 946/.6--dc23
LC record available at https://lccn.loc.gov/2016017872[lccn.loc.gov]

Contents

Note on Basque Orthography

The standard form to refer to the Basque language today is Euskara. Most English-language texts on the Basque Country have traditionally employed only the French and Spanish orthographic renderings of Basque place names. Here, in light of the standard Basque orthographic renderings of these same place names by the Basque Language Academy (Euskaltzaindia), we will endeavor to use these Basque versions, with an addition in parentheses of the French or Spanish equivalents on first mention in each chapter.

Some exceptions to this rule include the use of Navarre (Nafarroa in Basque, Navarra in Spanish) and Lower Navarre (Nafarroa Beherea in Basque, Basse Navarre in French); the hyphenated bilingual cases of Donostia-San Sebastián, Vitoria-Gasteiz, and Iruñea-Pamplona; and occasions where French or Spanish place name variants are used to make a linguistic point. In the latter case, the Basque equivalents appear in parentheses after the French or Spanish place name.

Additionally, on occasion we anglicize certain Basque terms, rather than use the original Basque, French, or Spanish terms themselves. Thus, for example, inhabitants of Zuberoa (Soule), instead of being rendered as *zuberotarrak* or *xiberotarrak* (from the Basque alternative Xiberoa), or *Souletines* (in French), are described here as Zuberoans.

It should be noted that, for much of the period under study here, there was little consistency in the rendering of either place names or personal names in any of these languages; a fact of life that is apparent in a region of Europe where multiple cultures and identities overlap. We see such lack of consistency as a more flexible way of appreciating this diversity.

Introduction

Beñat Oyharçabal

In recent decades, many French speakers have first come to know about the Basques through Jacques Allières's concise, reliable book, which we now publish in English for the first time. The book is part of the Presses Universitaires de France's well-known collection *Que sais-je?* (What do I know about . . . ?) and follows the publishers' established criteria: namely, a specialist provides concise information for the general reader about a particular subject in a 128-page, small-format book (12x18 cm). In 2013, there were more than 3,650 books in the collection, one of which is Allières's *The Basques*, about the Basque Country and its inhabitants.

Verbal Morphology

Born in Toulouse in 1929, and dying in 2000 in the same region, Allières was a Romance linguist who also studied Basque and became an expert in this language, and was even appointed an honorary academician of Euskaltzaindia, the Royal Academy of the Basque Language. He completed his secondary and university education in his hometown. He then passed the *agrégation* (a competitive examination to enter French public service) as a French grammar teacher, thus obtaining the highest teaching qualification in France, in 1954. He took up a teaching position in Baiona (Bayonne) the same year, which is where he first came into contact with Basque speakers. However, shortly afterward he was involved in a car accident and had to return to Toulouse, where he started to lecture on French linguistics at the university and worked on his dissertation about Gascon: *Dialectic and Synchronic Description of the Gascon Verb*. Meanwhile, he carried on studying Basque, with the young Basque seminarians at Institut Catholique proving to be useful sources of information for his research. He asked each one of them to translate the parable of the Prodigal Son into the language as spoken in each of their villages.

While he knew Classical languages well, he was, above all, a Romance linguist. His published work in this area covers French and Catalan diachrony and Romance linguistics as well as Gascon and Occitan in general. However, colleagues who knew him best were aware that his curiosity about languages and their diversity had led him to acquire knowledge about a great number of languages outside his specialized area, including Indo-European, Semitic, Chinese, and Finno-Ugric languages.[1] He developed this curiosity at a very young age, including his interest in Basque, making Pierre Lafitte's Basque grammar book his bedside reading as an adolescent.[2]

Without any doubt, when it came to non-Romance languages, Allières focused mostly on Basque, as evinced by that part of his considerable published work dedicated to the language.[3] His interest in Basque seems to have been aroused partly by the exotic nature of the language in the Romance context and, more generally, in the Indo-European context of the whole continent, a factor which had also attracted other non-native speaker linguists; another factor was the possibility that the language might have had particular connections with Gascon in the past. Romance linguist Gerhard Rohlfs had worked extensively since before World War II on the linguistics around historian Achille Luchaire's hypothesis (1875/1877, 1879) that the divinities mentioned in the Latin inscriptions found in Aquitaine dating from the first century

---

1. This book was published as volume 5 of the *Atlas linguistique et ethnographique de la Gascogne*, an extensive work begun and directed by Jean Séguy.

2. Lafitte, *Grammaire basque, dialecte bas-navarrais-labourdin*.

3. A first list of works about Basque can be found in Videgain, "Travaux de Jacques Allières sur le domaine basque."

C.E. must have been connected with Basque.[4] Allières also believed that the Gascon linguistic area was, in fact, the Latinized part of Aquitaine where Proto-Basque had previously been spoken, and that this could explain the existence of certain particular features in Gascon in the more general Occitan context.[5]

From the theoretical point of view, Allières was a member of the generation in which André Martinet's structuralism dominated linguistics in France. He followed this functionalist current throughout his career, paying particular attention to dialectic variety and polymorphism.[6] His most important work on Basque can be divided into two areas. On the one hand, study into particular subjects such as verb form structure, little known documents about dialectology, and questions relating to Basque-Gascon; and on the other, work aimed at making Basque better known to the general public, and particularly this book, which we have now translated into English.

Work on Verb Morphology

Allière's work on verb morphology is a continuation of René Lafon's work from a typically systematically organized and classified structuralist perspective. In a 1979 article titled "Statut et fonction de formes verbales pluripersonnelles" (Status and function of multipersonal verb forms) Allières studies verb morphology in various languages, including Basque, Ainu, Swahili, Quechua, Georgian, and Northwestern Caucasian languages, with regard to syntactical argument indexation.[7] He also aimed to demonstrate, on the one hand, the diversity of linguistic models including multipersonal inflections and, on the other, to underline the scarcity of

---

4. See Rohlfs, *Le gascon*. See also Luchaire, *Les origines linguistiques de l'Aquitaine*.

5. For farther work on the hypothesis that Proto-Gascon was a Romance language built on a Basque substrate, see Chambon and Greub, "Note sur l'âge du (proto) gascon."

6. See Allières, "Dialectologie et fonctionnalisme."

7. Allières, "Statut et fonction de formes verbales pluripersonnelles."

variation observed in the syntactic structures associated with this phenomenon in contrast to their varied morphology.

The conclusion of his work on Basque verb morphology is to be found in his definitive essay published originally in 1982: "De la formalisation du système verbal basque" (On the formalization of the Basque verb system).[8] Since the mid-eighteenth century, and particularly after Louis-Lucien Bonaparte and Emmanuel Inchauspé's work in the following century, work on Basque verb forms has been many Basque grammarians' chosen area of study. Allières contributed toward the modern classification of Basque verb forms, and the essential points he made are still to be found in current works, notably in those of Euskaltzaindia's Grammar Commission.[9] In order to establish the basis for this classification, Allières believed that four pitfalls should be avoided: importing categories from neighboring languages that would only lead to confusion and errors; taking only one speaker into account, which might put the system's uniqueness at risk; the semantic, nonformal definition of concessive clauses as a basis for classifying forms that, he believed, would give rise to many difficulties, particularly taking into account the lability of certain modal markers such as -*ke*; an overly rigorous differentiation between verb morphology in itself and syntactic morphology, in other words, the morphology of affixes associated with subordinate clauses. In fact, until then most grammars had included verb forms with a complementary suffix, traditionally known as the connective suffix (-*(e)n*) and with the conditional prefix *ba-* as specific verb forms, which leads to a multiplication of verb patterns.

Allières made use of the oldest existing Basque grammar, that of Pierre Urte (1714), to construct his analysis grid for verb pat-

---

8. Allières, "De la formalisation du système verbal basque."
9. See *Euskal Gramatikaren Lehen Urratsak.*

terns.[10] In his grammar, Urte offers a rich variety and profusion of verb patterns, but he was not really a grammarian and set verb patterns on the basis of clitic personal pronouns from French. This leads to a certain confusion with regard to purely formal variations, in other words, polymorphism in the strict sense, as well as in the relevant synonyms and in connection with different lexical items.

Work on Dialectic Variation and Phenomena Arising from Contact between Basque and Gascon

Having written his dissertation as part of a linguistic atlas, Allières remained interested in dialectic variations throughout his career, and this can also be seen in his work on Basque. He was particularly interested in material that had been almost ignored until then in spite of its significance. Specifically, he looked at two collections of short texts published in Iparralde (the Northern Basque Country) at the end of the nineteenth century: the first was carried out by Julien Sacaze (1847–1889),[11] who asked school teachers in all the local boroughs of the eight *départements* in the Pyrenees, including the Northern Basque Country, to translate two local legends; the second was carried out by a Romance linguist, Edouard Bourciez (1854–1946), who, after being appointed professor of Language and Literature of the South-West at the University of Bordeaux in 1895, researched ways of speech in Gascony, asking schoolteachers in five *départements* in the South-West to translate the parable

10. Urte, "Statut et limite du polymorphisme morphologique: le verbe dans la Grammaire cantabrique basque de Pierre d'Urte (1712), première partie," and "Statut et limite du polymorphisme morphologique: le verbe dans la Grammaire cantabrique basque de Pierre d'Urte (1712), seconde partie (les auxiliaires)."

11. Sacaze, *Recueil de linguistique et de toponymie des Pyrénées.* Texts from boroughs in the Basque Country are included in volume 1 (taken from the district of Baiona) and volume 2 (district of Maule [Mauléon]). These texts are available online at: http://numerique.bibliotheque.toulouse.fr/ark:/74899/B315556101_MS1110 and http://numerique.bibliotheque.toulouse.fr/ark:/74899/B315556101_MS1111.

of the Prodigal Son into their local ways of speech.[12] In the early 1960s, Allières published the results of his initial research into the Basque texts in Lacaze's collection, and later published two works on the texts in Bourciez's collection.[13]

Allières also researched the connections between Gascon and Basque, and more specifically Gascon in the wider Occitan context and its parallelisms with Basque, mainly phonetically and phonologically, and, to a lesser extent, morphologically, and, to an even lesser extent, syntactically.[14] Starting from the idea that the Gascons and Vascones were descended from the same ethnic group, he observed that the linguistic structures in each of these languages were, nevertheless, radically different, it being difficult to find Gascon particularities that point to a substrate effect beyond the characteristics already pointed out by Rohlfs.[15]

Summaries

Allières's two summaries about the Basques and their language are probably connected. In fact, his *Manuel pratique de basque* (Practical manual of Basque, 1979)[16] seems to have been based on material he collected for his book *Les Basques* (The Basques), which he had published two years earlier, and later expanded. Both works were

---

12. Bourciez, *Recueil des idiomes de la région Gascogne*, unpublished ms. Most of this collection has not been published. It is very extensive, being comprised of 17 volumes, with translations collected in almost 4,500 boroughs. The 150 manuscripts of the Basque texts have recently been published and mapped. See Aurrekoetxea and Videgain, *Haur prodigoaren parabola Ipar Euskal Herriko 150 bertsiotan*, available at: http://artxiker.ccsd.cnrs.fr/index.php?halsid=n3ahmddmaba49g0jbvip30bqc1&view_this_doc=artxibo-00086827&version=1. See also Aurrekoetxea, Videgain, and Iglesias, Bourciez bildumako euskal atlasa (BBEA): 1. Lexikoa" and "Bourciez bildumako euskal atlasa (BBEA): 2. Gramatikoa."

13. Allières, "Petit atlas linguistique basque français Sacaze I," and "Petit atlas linguistique basque français Bourciez (I)."

14. Allières, "Gascón y euskera: afinidades e interrelaciones lingüísticas."

15. A recent work, makes use of Allières's published and unpublished work on Gascon. See Massoure, *Le Gascon, les mots et le système*.

16. Allières, *Manuel pratique de basque*.

written taking non-Basque speakers into account and they were his main target readership.

Manuel pratique de basque is didactic and designed for readers with good linguistic knowledge. After explaining the pre-historical period, the history of the study of Basque, and Basque grammar, more than half of the work is an anthology of texts. There are twenty short texts by various authors in various dialects, genres, and periods, which are also translated and accompanied by sentence-by-sentence linguistic commentaries.

Les Basques is the work presented here, translated into English. Unlike *Manuel pratique de basque*, and although Allières was a linguist, this work is not entirely about the language. In fact, as the title suggests, it is a book about the Basque Country and its inhabitants. The first edition was published in 1977 and the most edition recent dates from 2003. The sixth edition, in 1999, was the last to be corrected and expanded. Be that as it may, events most closely connected to changes in society are of marginal importance in this work, which is based on the Basque Country's most durable features and particularly its language.

As Allières states in his introduction, offering information about the Basques in such a limited format is almost impossible. He does so by giving the reader useful information in each section without reducing the high standard of his academic texts, as befits a book that is part of an encyclopaedic project, particularly in connection, directly or indirectly, with the language. In fact, while this book offers little information about items of contemporary culture, that is not the work's main subject: it is more centered on ethnology and anthropology, which is why the language takes such a prominent place, the Basques themselves using it to denominate their own ethnic group.

From a linguistic point of view, this book follows Lafon's classic line except with regards to passive verbs.[17] It should also be pointed out that, unlike in most traditional grammars, the term "declension" is not used to designate inflections, although Allières

---

17. Lafon, *Le système du verbe basque au XVIe siècle*.

does use the verb "decline," in quotation marks, to describe noun and adjective inflections. The ergative structure is described, and the non-marked case is described as nominative (and not as absolutive), without associating it with either an active or a passive voice, consistent with his idea that there is no such theoretical difference in the language and, consequently, that using such terms is inappropriate. The adnominal suffix *–ko* is analyzed by using the traditional term "genitive locative" rather than as a complementary morpheme.

In his explanation of conjugated verbs, Allières distinguishes the personal markers connected with multipersonal verb inflections and terms them "drawers," in other words verbal indicators that express modes and tenses. His analysis of periphrastic verbs stands out. He describes the four auxiliary verbs, but defines the lexical verbs that are also auxiliary verbs (*edun* 'to have' and *izan* 'to be') as *nominal forms* or *invariable adjectival forms*, which is reminiscent of the oldest theories in which Basque verbs are very reduced in scope: consequently, he does not make use of the category of grammatical aspect in order to explain their combinations.

Allières takes a primarily morphological approach and certain questions, such as those connected with sentence order, are not dealt with at any length. In this regard, he limits himself to mentioning the general complement > verb order, with the exception of attributive adjectives. For example, he does not mention the consequences of the structure of information in this respect, although this subject was well known, especially following the work of Seber Altube.[18]

Allières was writing in the late 1970s, on the eve of a decade in which Basque syntactic research was to undergo remarkable development.[19] So it is no surprise that the underlying theoretical approach to Basque morphosyntaxis in this book may seem a little

---

18. Altube, 1929.

19. The work undertaken in the 1970s was much influenced by the publication of Patxi Goenaga's grammar *Gramatika bideetan* (1978). As well as being the first grammar to be entirely drawn up and written in Basque, it is a work prepared in the context of generative grammar.

out-of-date in some respects, particularly with regard to syntax. It is also true that dealing with such a subject in a short work, aimed at a nonspecialist readership, is difficult. But his discussion of morphology, which was his specialist area, is still largely relevant.

The reader, then, should consider the text in that historical context. We have spoken about the linguistic part of the book, which was the author's main subject of interest, being a linguist himself. The book is of equal, if not greater value for its sections on contemporary history and about particular cultural activities. It was initially written before the post-Franco constitution (1978) came into force, and, of course, before the creation of autonomous communities in Spain.[20] It should also be taken into account that the University of the Basque Country had not yet been founded and it was this university, in fact, which was to develop Basque studies in general and Basque linguistics so considerably. While this may seem obvious, there is no doubt that Allières's work is a good portrait of Basque studies in the late 1970s, seeing the whole of the Basque Country from its northern side.

References

Allières, Jacques. "Petit atlas linguistique basque français Sacaze I." *Via Domitia* 7 (1960): 205–11, + 15 maps.

———. "Petit atlas linguistique basque français Bourciez (I)." *Fontes Linguae Vasconum* 27 (1977): 353–86.

———. "Statut et fonction de formes verbales pluripersonnelles." *La linguistique* 15, no. 1 (1979): 3–30.

———. *Manuel pratique de basque*. Collection Connaissance des langues, vol. 13. Paris: Picard, 1979.

———. "Gascón y euskera: Afinidades e interrelaciones lingüísticas." *Anuario del Seminario de Filología Vasca Julio de Urquijo* 26, no. 3 (1992): 801–11.

---

20. The later editions deal, to some extent, with more recent changes but the work and its general approach have not really been influenced by subsequent updates.

———. "Dialectologie et fonctionnalisme." *La linguistique* 31, no. 2 (1996): 15–31.

———. "De la formalisation du système verbal basque." In *Piarres Lafitte-ri omenaldia*. IKER 2. Bilbao: Euskaltzaindia, 2003. Altube. 1929.

Aurrekoetxea, Gotzon, and Xarles Videgain. *Haur prodigoaren parabola Ipar Euskal Herriko 150 bertsiotan*. Anuario del Seminario Julio de Urquijo supplement 49. Leioa: UPV, Servicio Editorial/EHU, Argitalpen Zerbitzua, 2004.

Aurrekoetxea, Gotzon, Xarles Videgain, and Aitor Iglesias. "Bourciez bildumako euskal atlasa (BBEA): 1. Lexikoa." *Anuario del Seminario Julio de Urquijo* 38, no. 2 (2004): 1–309.

———. "Bourciez bildumako euskal atlasa (BBEA): 2. Gramatikoa." *Anuario del Seminario Julio de Urquijo* 39, no. 1 (2005): 1–277.

Chambon, Jean-Pierre, and Yan Greub "Note sur l'âge du (proto) gascon." *Revue de linguistique romane* 66 (July–December 2002): 473–95.

Euskal Gramatikaren Lehen Urratsak. 7 volumes. Bilbao: Euskaltzaindia, 1985–2011.

Goenaga, Patxi. *Gramatika bideetan*. Donostia: Erein, 1978.

Lafitte, Pierre. *Grammaire basque, dialecte bas-navarrais-labourdin*. 1944; Second revised and expanded edition, Bayonne: Ikas, 1962.

Lafon, René. *Le système du verbe basque au XVIe siècle*. 1944; facsimile edition, Bayonne: Elkar, 1980.

Luchaire, Achille. *Les origines linguistiques de l'Aquitaine*. Pau, 1877.

———. *Etudes sur les idiomes pyrénéens de la région française*. Paris: Maisonneuve, 1879; reprint, Genève: Slatkine, 1973.

Massoure, Jean-Louis. *Le Gascon, les mots et le système*. Paris: Honoré Champion, 2012.

Rohlfs, Gerhard. *Le gascon*. 1935; 3rd expanded edition, Tübingen: Max Niemeyer and Pau: Marrimpouey jeune, 1977.

Sacaze, Julien. *Recueil de linguistique et de toponymie des Pyrénées.* 35 volumes. 1887.

Séguy, Jean, ed. *Atlas linguistique et ethnographique de la Gascogne.* 6 volumes. Paris: Editions du CNRS, 1954–1973.

Urte, Pierre. "Statut et limite du polymorphisme morphologique: le verbe dans la Grammaire cantabrique basque de Pierre d'Urte (1712), première partie." In *Symbolae Ludovico Mitxelena septuagenario oblatae.* Volume 2. Vitoria-Gasteiz: Instituto de Ciencias de la Antiguedad, UPV/Aintzinate-Zientzien Institutoa, EHU, 1985.

―――. "Statut et limite du polymorphisme morphologique: le verbe dans la Grammaire cantabrique basque de Pierre d'Urte (1712), seconde partie (les auxiliaires)." In *Anuario del Seminario Julio de Urquijo*, Supplement 14, no. 2 (1991): 767–812.

Videgain, Xarles. "Travaux de Jacques Allières sur le domaine basque." *Lapurdum* 5 (2000): 9–11.

The Basques

Jacques Allières

Part 1

Geographical Context

1

Location

The Basque Country includes and flanks the most westerly part of
the Pyrenees mountain range. Its boundaries go from Auñamendi
Mountain in the east to the Nerbioi [Nervión] River in the west,
from the Aturri [Adour] River in the north to the Toloño Mountains in the south; in other words, between 0°14'15" in the east and
2°57'40" in the west, 43°25' in the north and 42°50 in the south.

In France, the Basque Country and the Basque language
have the same boundaries, running along the Ühaitza [Saison]
River, carrying along the Oloron River, which flows to the east
of Santa Grazi [Sainte-Engrâce], Eskiula [Esquiüle], Ospitalepea
[L'Hôpital-Saint-Blaise], Sarrikotapea [Charritte-de-Bas], Arüe
[Aroue] (Montori [Montory], to the west of Ereta [Arette], is bilin-
gual); the boundary crosses the Biduze [Bidouze], a tributary of
the Aturri, downstream from Donapaleu [Saint Palais]; it crosses
Arrueta [Arraute] and Bardoze [Bardos], goes through Bastida
[Labastide-Clairence] (which is bilingual) and between Beskoitze
[Briscous] and the Aturri; it turns south at Baiona and Biarritz,
where it reaches the Bay of Biscay.

The situation in Spain is more complicated due to the old language's fast and continual retreat: while the provinces of Bizkaia
[Vizcaya], Araba [Álava], and Gipuzkoa [Guipúzcoa] are said to
be "Basquified" (*Vascongadas*), and Navarre is one of the oldest
bastions of Euskara [the Basque language], the current linguistic frontier, from west to east, leaves out Bilbao and runs from
Legutio [Villarreal] in Araba, follows the boundary of Gipuzkoa
(which is the only province that is still entirely Basque-speaking),

and goes to the north of Altsasu [Alsasua], Irurtzun [Irurzun], and Pamplona-Iruñea, leaving Basque in only the high Pyrenean valleys to the north before meeting the French border in the north-east of the Erronkari [Roncal] Valley. However, the whole of the area in which place names are still clearly Basque can be called the "Spanish Basque Country," from Vitoria-Gasteiz and Lizarra [Estella] to Pamplona-Iruñea and the towns around it, Irunberri [Lumbier], Nabaskoze [Navascués], and the upper Erronkari, to the north of Salvatierra [in the province of Zaragoza].

2

Human and Political Geography

In this chapter we will examine political geography: see part 2 and part 4 for information about human geography.

In Spain the Basque-speaking country includes, from west to east, the *"Vascongada"* provinces: Bizkaia (2,197 km²; 716,513 inhabitants),[1] whose capital is Bilbao and whose main towns are Durango, Markina (Marquina), and Gernika (Guernica); Araba (3,044 km², 172,198 inhabitants), capital Vitoria-Gasteiz, other main town Guardia [Laguardia]; Gipuzkoa (1,844 km², 445,198 inhabitants), capital Donostia-San Sebastián, main towns Irun, Eibar, Tolosa, Azpeitia, Bergara [Vergara]. Tha capital of Navarre (10,506 km², 502,875 inhabitants) is Pamplona-Iruñea, main towns Agoitz [Aoiz], Tafalla, Lizarra, Tutera [Tudela], Erriberri [Olite].

In France, the Basque "provinces" are all in the Baiona and Oloron districts within the Pyrénées-Atlantiques *département*: Lapurdi [Labourd] (777 km², 144,213 inhabitants), capital Uztaritze [Ustaritz], main towns Baiona (which is only partially Basque), Biarritz, Donibane Lohizune [Saint-Jean-de-Luz], Ezpeleta [Espelette], Ainhoa, Hendaia [Hendaye]; Lower Navarre (1,500 km², 32,000 inhabitants), capital Donibane Garazi [Saint-Jean-Pied-de-Port], main towns Kanbo [Cambo-les-Bains], Baigorri [Saint-Etienne-de-Baïgorry], Iholdi [Iholdy], Hazparne [Hasparren], Bastida, Donapaleu; Zuberoa [Soule] (817 km², 17,167 inhabitants), captial Maule, other main town Atharratze [Tardets].

---

1. Figures are taken from Canon Pierre Lafitte's article "Basques" in the *Encyclopaedia Universalis*.

The Spanish-French border follows the mountain crests except at six places where old local economy arrangements (see "grazing rights and agreements") or cartographic convenience have taken priority: from east to west, part of the forest of Irati [Iraty] on the southern side of the mountain range belongs to France; Luzaide [Valcarlos], on the northern side, belongs to Spain; the people of Baigorri have the right to use the pasture land in Kintoa [Pays Quint in French; Quinto Real in Spanish], which, itself, belongs to Spain despite being on the northern side of the mountains; Baztan, the upper basin of the Bidasoa, belongs to Spain; in Bortziriak [Cinco Villas] the border follows natural boundaries (rivers and forests).

The border between the Basque Country and Béarn follows the old road between the Erronkari and Baretos Valleys, the Ereta Pass being the boundary between France and Spain.[2]

---

2. See J. Sermet, "La délimitation de la frontière de Navarre," in *Melanges offerts à G. Viers* (Toulouse, 1975), pp. 477–497.

Part 2

From the Origins to the Present

Prehistory

With no linguistic remains from the most remote periods, is it realistic to hope to find some trace of the Basque race, which defines itself in terms of its language, in paleolithic or neolithic burial sites? Perhaps this human group, which was undoubteldy fairly homogeneous at the start of its historical period, was isolated precisely because of its language at the time when Western Europe was being flooded by incoming Indo-European language speakers.

There are numerous prehistorical sites across the Basque Country and excavations are continually uncovering new pieces of personal property, made both of stone and of other materials, and human bones, particularly skulls, which, having been systematically measured, show a remarkable degree of continuity in local inhabitants.

There are no Stone Age remains prior to the Middle Paleolithic period.

The stone tools found protected under the rock of Olha (near Kanbo), in Hiriburu [Saint-Pierre-d'Irube], in the caves at Izturitze [Isturitz], in Altzürükü [Aussurucq] (Pyrénées-Atlantiques), and in Zuñiga (to the west of Lizarra in Spanish Navarre) are from the Mousterian period, as is the Neandertahl jawbone found in Izturitze.

Considerably later than the strata excavations in South-West France (see F. Jordá), remains found at Sara [Sare], Ozaze [Ossas], Hiriburu, Izturitze, and Santimamiñe (Bizkaia) have been dated as late Mousterian, contemporary with the Aurignacian culture and French Périgordian and, therefore, Upper Paleolithic. Soultrean

remains have been found in Izturitze and Santimamiñe, as well as
those at Mouligna beach in Biarritz, in Altzürükü and Bolinkoba
(Bizkaia), and Ermitia (Gipuzkoa); Magdalenian remains have
been found in Santimamiñe, Bolinkoba, Izturitze, and Ermitia, as
well as in Aitzbitarte, Urtiaga (Gipuzkoa), Lumentxa, Baltzola,
and Armiña (Bizkaia). Paleolithic cave paintings have been found
at Izturitze, Alkerdi (Navarre), Atxerri, Santimamiñe, and Goiko-
lau (Bizkaia), and sculptured objects at Izturitze, Berroberria,
Aitzbitarte, Urtiaga, Ermitia, Lumentxa, Santimamiñe, Atxeta,
Bolinkoba, Arezti, and Atxuri (Bizkaia). Epipalelithic remains have
been found with Azilian features at all of the above places (except
for Aitzbitarte, Lezetxiki, Altxerri, and Atxeta) and also at Berroberria. Remains from the transition from the Magdalenian to the
Azilian have also been found at Silibranka (Bizkaia) and Lamine-
neskatza (Gipuzkoa), an isolated find.

Without spending time examining the nature and characteristics of these material cultures, which are secondary to our subject
and fully covered in specialist works, let us underline the fact that
the skulls found at these sites are mostly of the "Western Pyrenean" class, which is also true of contemporary Basques. This
type of skull, which can be described as Cro-Magnon modified by
basion introversion (front edge of the occipital cavity), is found
in most neolithic burial sites. These archeological findings, which
date from prehistory, are unbroken. They are to be found at Santimamiñe, Lumentxa, Ermitia, Urtiaga, Balzola, Berroberria, and
numerous other sites. The middens found at some sites provide evidence of this new type of existence but ceramics, which are usually
found at such sites, have only been found from later dates.

Then, even before the Bronze Age, the "Megalithic idea"
reached the Basque Country, apparently connected with funeral
rites, brought by new inhabitants from the east and the south.
Three waves can be distinguished (J. Maluquer de Motes): the first
can be seen in the dolmens erected in the mountain ranges and pasture lands of the "classic" type (Gorbea, Aitzgorri, Urbasa, Aralar,
Larraun, and Abodi in Spain; Larun, Artzamendi, the Iholdi area,
the high ground between the Errobi River and the Ühaitza Rivers

in France) and the "corridor tombs" (lower Araba and mid-Navarre); the second type can be seen in the great covered galleries at Artaxoa [Artajona] (Navarre); the third type is to be found in Erronkari Valley and is similar to that in the Catalan Pyrenees.

The Basque Country seems to have been very open and receptive to different cultures at that time and also to waves of incoming populations, which seems to contradict traditional views about the Basques. While the "western Pyrenean" racial type we have described above is still predominant, it is mixed not only with Mediterranean types, of which there are many, but also with some brachycephalic Alpine and Armenoid types. The latter appeared during the Iron Age, thereby constituting the most influential of these ethnic migrations: the Indo-Europeans. It seems that these people, who may have been Celts, went through the Basque Country without stopping there, on their way to the western Iberian peninsular. But the prolonged contact that the indigenous people had with the invaders was sufficient for the former to acquire new technical knowledge such as working with iron, animal traction, perhaps new agricultural processes and crops and, undoubtedly, cattle and horse raising techniques, which had scarcely been present beforehand. It is probably also from this time that the first Celtic influences affected the Basque language (see below).

2

Protohistory

While many of the previous conclusions are based on fact, the following chapter is going to make use of writings from antiquity and not just archaeology, which, from now on, will only be used to interpret or correct the former. The use that we will make of these writings is, in fact, the very definition of protohistory: finding about about people who did not use writing through contemporaries who did.

Documentary Basis: the Writings of Historians and Geographers in Antiquity

There are only two ways for us to research traces of the Basques in ancient sources: examining the toponymy[1] that they provide us with and detecting items that may be linked to the Basque language; and, in line with these sources, sketching the ethnic make-up of the areas inhabited by the Basques today as well as the surrounding areas enables us to try and see to what extent the comparason of ancient with current boundaries may yield information about the early settlements of proto-Basque or similar ethnic groups.

Ancient toponymy seems to give some solid points of reference: in some cases, the ancient names are exactly the same as current ones. It would be desirable to confirm toponymical iden-

---

1. Anthroponomy, limited as it is to the names of peoples, is of no use to us. Experience has shown that names are often those given to a people by their neighbors and that they are not the same as those that the people themselves use in their own language.

tifications with their archaeological counterparts, but this is not always absolutely certain. The modern town name Oiartzun can be seen in the ancient [Πομπαιλών]; Pamplona[2] (Basque *Iruñea*) can be seen in [-πέλών]; Calahorra can be seen in [Καλάγουρις]/ Calagur(r)is[3] (there are, in fact, other *Calagurris* in Spain, all called Calahorra now, and, in Southwest France, towns known as *Convenae* in ancient times (Saint-Martory, *département* number 31 [Haute-Garonne])); Arakil [Araquil] can be seen in ancient Araceli; in Aquitaine (see below), the inhabitants of *Ilumberris* (modern Auch) were the *Ausci*, a name reminiscent of the root for the Basque word for the Basque language: *eusk-* (*Euskara* = Basque), and so on. Unfortunately, many of the towns mentioned in ancient texts have either disappeared or changed name, and we do not know enough old names of many existant towns.

Let us now look at the information provided by writers in antiquity about the geography of the Basque Country.

South of the Pyrenees, the Greek Polybius (2nd century BCE, *Fragments historiques*, Historical fragments, III) and, above all, Strabo (66 BCE – 24 CE, [Γεωλραφία] III) and Ptolemy (mid-second century, [Γεωγραφία] III) allow us to place the peoples (who we will name here in Latin) in the area between the Nerbioi (in Bizkaia) and the Gállego rivers (in the province of Huesca) and south to approximately the current boundaries of Navarre and Araba.

The Caristii inhabited Bizkaia and part of Araba to just south of Vitoria-Gasteiz; the Varduli inhabited Gipuzkoa and another part of Araba to just north of Guardia; the Vascones inhabited Navarre, northern Aragón, and the province of Huesca to the River Gállego as well as eastern Araba; the Berones inhabited almost the whole of the rest of Araba; the Autrigones inhabited the lands farther west up to the Bay of Biscay.

---

2. This means the "(Great) Town of Pompey." Pompaei + *ilun* (cf. *Irun*) may be the augmentative form of *(h)iri* = town (see below). In Basque, Pamplona is *Iruñea*, which simply means "the large town."

3. [Γραχουρις]/Graccur(r)is, which no longer exists, is a town name formed in the same way, based on the personal name Tiberius Sempronius Gracchus, "Gracchus's Town" (*uri* is a western variant of *iri*).

We will not use any farther Greek or Latin documents with information about this subject because they are often full of contradictions. Greek writers include Plutarch, a contemporary of Strabo's, and others from the third century; the main Latin writers include Sallust (first century BCE), Isidore of Seville (sixth–seventh century), Livy, Pliny the Elder, Pomponius Mela, Tacitus, the invaluable Avienus (*Ora Maritima*, fourth century), Ausonius, Ammianus Marcellinus, and Prudentius.

North of the Pyrenees, while the aforementioned writers provide invaluable information, it is Caesar himself who gives us most information, stating in a famous passage in his *Gallic War* (*De bello gallico*, I, 1), that the Aquitanians inhabited the land between the River Garonne, the Pyrenees, and the Bay of Biscay. This area is certainly wider than that of the "French" Basque Country, but we will see below how essential this record was.

Possible Interpretations

We must distinguish carefully between certainties and asumptions.

One Certain Fact: the Basques had no connection with the Celts. The language may have borrowed some words and perhaps its vigesimal number system from Celtic languages, there may have been certain traits in common between the proto-Basques and the Celts, their nearest neighbors, without this placing in doubt the value of the formula "ethnic group equals language," particularly during the protohistorical period. It will be observed that the writers of the time, who knew the Celts well, were careful to distinguish the borders between them and the peoples mentioned earlier, both north and south of the Pyrenees.

We will return to the Aquitanian problem later; to the south, onomastics (cf. J. Untermann) confirm classical writers' reports very clearly, having no doubt in designating an "Iberian" area (the southeastern half of the peninsular) and a completely separate "Celtic" area (the northwestern half).

Facts are not so clear with regard to the relationship between the proto-Basques and the Iberians. Archaeology tells us that the lands inhabited by the Caristii, the Varduli, and the Vascones, as well as Aquitaine, were not part of Iberian civilization.

As the historical texts are not clear on this point, we must look to linguistic evidence to see if it confirms the archaeological findings. From this point of view, while some terms or "bases" allow us to establish parallels between them (we quote first the Iberian and then the Basque: *and-/handi* 'big'; *baes-/bas(o)* 'wood, wild'; *-bels/ beltz* 'black'; *il(t)i/(h)iri* 'town'; *il(d)un/ilun* 'shadow') they are very few when held up to considerable and unquestionable evidence to the contrary.

Since M. Gómez ("La escritura ibérica," in *Boletín de la Real Academia de la Historia*, 1943) discovered the key to Iberian writing (an unusual combination of an alphabetic and syllabic systems), we are able to read all the inscriptions left behind by the Iberians and the Celtiberians. While inscriptions in the Celtiberian areas (probably written by people of Celtic origin and in Celtic languages, the people having adapted to Iberian civilization) are unquestionably Indo-European (translations have been suggested for some of them), those from Iberian areas are reminiscent of no other known language and remain indecipherable enigmas. However, we should state once more that these later inscriptions do have a certain linguistic air in common with Basque in the structure of the words and in certain suffixes; perhaps there was a distant relationship between the two languages, but any direct derivation from one to the other can be ruled out completely.

In fact, the letters *il(t)i-* create an interesting problem; they are often combined with a second series of letters, *ber(r)i*: cf. the Basque *hiri* 'town' and *berri* 'new'. This combination is often to be found not only in Basque and Aquitanian place names (for instance, *Iluro*, Oloron; *Eliberris*, Auch; *Ilumberris*, Irunberri [Navarre]), but also in areas that were part of Iberian civilization (*Iltida*, Lleida; *Cauco Iliberris*, Collioure; *Iliberris*, Elne; *Iluro*, Mataró, near Barcelona; and even *Iliberris*, Granada, in Andalusia). Perhaps this combination was so frequent because it was a name to be expected, like Newtown (Villeneuve, Neustadt, Neápolis, Novgorod, Noviodunum, and so on), and it spread to Iberian areas thanks to the possible distant relationship between the two languages; or perhaps our approach to whole issue is inappropriate because of our lack of information.

The question is farther complicated when we look into the Iberians' possible origins. One classic theory posits their homeland in North Africa, linking them with the oldest inhabitants of that region, the Berbers (with the names of both people being constructed on the same root, *ber*).

Linguists who examine the origins of Basque also tend to favor one of two basic hypotheses. One of them is based on certain features of the language that have similarities with Semitic languages (Berber, for example); the second is the Caucasian hypothesis. In fact, if one sought to rely not just on the "undeniable" evidence provided by archeologists and linguists, this second approach seems to answer all the questions, as we will see later.

Having mentioned the difficulty of understanding the relationship between the "proto-Basques" and their neighbors in antiquity, a difficulty that we will examine with greater perspective later on, we will now try to better identify these people whose geographical location seems to define them as such. The central ethnic group was the Vascones, from whose name both "Basque" and "Gascon" are derived, and who inhabited what is today Navarre[4] (in the twelfth century the French pilgrim Aimeric Picaud, on his way to Compostela, wrote in his famous *Codex Calixtinus* that the "Basques" (*Bascli*) lived in the mountains, particularly to the north, and the Navarrese (*Navarri*) inhabited the plain toward Pamplona-Iruñea: this is undoubtely the first historical reference to distinctions between two groups that had previously been one. See below).

As we have said, the Vascones of Navarre's western neighbors were the Varduli, who had the Caristii for neighbors. The historical and dialectical division between the provinces of Gipuzkoa and

---

4. Curiously, A. Tovar suggests an Indo-European etymology for this name, believing it to derive from *bhars-* (height), which would make the Vascones mountain people or, figuratively, haughty or proud (cf. the inscription *barscunes/bascunes* on coins from antiquity, origin unknown).

Bizkaia points to these two peoples being their respective ances-
tors, and those of the Basques themselves, although already politi-
cally one with the Vascones, which is why the Spaniards call these
provinces "vascongadas," in other words, "Basquified."

The origins of Araba, whose name does not seem to be Iberian or old Basque, are less clear. The names of the Autrigones
and Berones, the western and southern neighbors of the Caristii,
Varduli, and Vascones, "sound" Celtic, which is confirmed by writers from antiquity and by archaeology.

With regard to the current names of the "Basquified" provinces, Bizkaia undoubtedly comes from *bizkar* (spine), meaning,
by extension, "mountain crest." Gipuzkoa derives from the antho-
ponym *(G)iputz*. The name Nafarroa (Navarre) brings to mind the
Basque word *naba* (plain) (cf. Aimeric Picaud).

Having described "'Vasconia" to the south of the Pyrenees, we
now turn to the northern area, where our interpretations will have
to rely even more heavily on hypotheses that, in our view, are highly
credible. When Caesar differentiated between Aquitaine and the
lands inhabited by the Celts, he defined the region that historians
and linguists all call "Gascony"... *Vasconia*!

The Pyrenees–Garonne–Bay of Biscay triangle, with the addition of another triangle of land between the Garonne, the Pyrenees, and a straight line from Toulouse to Col de Port in Ariège
(this line is, in fact, the most precise isogloss boundary with regard
to the linguistics of Gascony), was, in general, carefully avoided
and bypassed by the Indo-European invaders during the Iron Age,
with one notable exception that explains certain misunderstand-
ings: during the early Iron Age, in the Neolithic period, some
"proto-Celts" did pass through this area and built Hallstat type
tumuli, many of them in the Pays de Buch (cf. Boii, "les Boïens"),
extending Celtic influence to the southwestern Gironde, along its
peripherie and along the Pyrenees (Bigorre, the Ger plateau, the
River Aturri, the high crests of the Aran valley in the Basque Country) and forming the Celtiberian ethnic group in Spain.

A second wave, with Hallstat characteristics according to G.
Fabre, and more clearly Celtic, reinforced the first wave's posi-

tion to the north of the Pyrenees. Toponyms bear witness to this Celtic presence in the Aran valley (*Salardú* from **Salar-dunum*, "place with abundance of trout"(?)), in Aragón (*Berdún* from **Virodunum*),5 without taking into account the Celtic names that Ptolemy, for instance, mentions around the whole periphery and even in what are today the "Vascongada" provinces; and we should remember at this point that the Autrigones and Berones seem to have been Celts.

To return to the issue of the ethnic make-up of Aquitaine, because linguistic criteria are still fully valid today and have been revealed to be accurate by research into Occitan dialectology,6 we will proceed to enumerate the characteristics that differentiate Gascon speakers from other Occitan speakers, restricting ourselves to phonetic considerations:

The old transformation of *f* into *h* (*filia* becomes *hilha* in Gascon, like the Spanish *hija* and unlike the Occitan *filha*);

The sound *v* is not used, being replaced by *b* (as in Spanish);

There is a contrast between simple and germinated consonants that leads to the disappearance of the letter *l* between vowels (*luna* (the moon) becomes *lua* in Gascon but is *luna* in Occitan) and the specific gemination of the Latin *ll* that becomes *r* between vowels (*bella* (beautiful) is *bera* in Gascon and *bela* in Occitan).

There is assimilation with the letter combinations *nd* and *mb* (**intendutum* [understood] is *entenut* in Gascon and *entendut* in Occitan); compare with the Catalan *segona* (second) derived from *secunda* and the Gaulish **cumba* (comb) leading to *coma*; also compare with the Spanish *paloma* (dove) derived from *palumba*;

There is vocalic prothesis before the intial letter *r* with stress (*rota* [wheel] is *arroda* in Gascon and *roda* in Occitan).

---

5. Also compare with the two towns called *Lugdunum*: L. Converarum (Saint Bertrand-de-Comminges, in *département* no. 31 [Haute-Garonne]) and *L. Consorannorum* (Saint-Lizier, *département* no. 09 [Ariège]). However, Lugdunum may be a "traveling toponym" in the same way that the Basque-Iberian placename *Iliberris* seems to have been.

6. Also published in the "Que sais-je?" collection. P. Bec (no. 1059).

This considerable body of differentiating characteristics is proably derived from the Aquitanians' own linguistic patterns.

Although we have no texts in their language (it would be very useful to have some), we are, nevertheless, able to form some idea of it thanks to the names of the divinities and people on inscriptions from the Gallo-Roman period to be found throughout western Gascony, from the boundaries of Zuberoa (Atharratze) to the southwest of Lot-et-Garonne (Sos) and Gascon Ariège (Saint-Girons). Among others, the words *Cison, Andere, Nescato*, and the combinations of letters *Sembe-* and *Bihos-* have been found and match Basque words exactly: *gizon* (man), *andere* (lady), *neskato* (young girl), *seme* (son), and *bihotz* (heart). There are other words whose meaning is less apparent, but which also sound like Basque: *Aherbelste, Astoilum, Baeserte, Ilurberrixo, Leherenn* and, in Atharratze, the celebrated inscription including the word *Herauscorritsehe*.

In addition to the town names derived from *ili-* and *ilun-*, which we have already mentioned, other Aquitanian names have been found on milestones: Bizkarrotze (in *département* no. 40 [Les Landes]) is clearly *bizkar* (see Bizkaia above); the "Aran" Valley in Spain is a Gascon name and identical to the Basque word for valley. We should also mention the many pre-Celtic and pre-Latin *-òs(se)* toponym endings and their variants that are exclusively Gascon (including those in the Aran Valley) and that seem to take the place of the analogous endings *-anum* (Latin) and *-acum* (Latinized Gaulish) farther to the east, except for some cases in Gers.

Most of the phonetic characteristics mentioned above have equivalent features in Basque:

In old Basque there is no letter *f*, and in contemporary Basque this letter only exists in loanwords from Latin or Romance languages. Words starting with *f* have the letter replaced by *p, b*, or *m*, depending on each local way of speech and each word.

There has never been a *v* in Basque: *b* is used in its place.

Anatem (duck) is *ahate* in Basque; *coronam* (crown) is *koroa*; *honoren* (honor) is *ohore*, and so on. When it comes to liquid consonants, *l* becomes *r* and *ll* becomes *l*: *voluntatem* (will) becomes *borondate*; *castelum* (castle), *gaztelu*.

The Roman **convitare* (invite) becomes *gomitatu*; in Spanish *convidar*, in French *convier*.

Rota (mill) becomes *errota*; *regem*, *errege*.

History (see the following chapter) agrees with this information, all of which leads us to believe that Caesar was referring to the proto-Basques when he wrote about Aquitanians. Most of Aquitaine (today Gascony) allowed itself to be Romanized, while the people in the far southwest (what is today the French Basque Country) remained loyal to their ancestral language.

Furthermore, certain minor linguistic features in Gascony near the border with Basque-speaking areas show farther connections between the two languages. There are areas (the Ossau, Aspe, and Barétous Valleys) in which intervocalic voiceless occlusives are still used as well as nasal stops (*cantata* becomes *candata*; *comperare*, *crombar*: cf. *cantada* and *crompar* in the rest of Gascony; in Basque, *gentem* (people) becomes *jende*; *tempora* (time), *denbora; seta* (silk), *zeta*; these same characteristics are to be found in northern Aragonese on the boundary between the Aran Valley and Basque-speaking areas), and perhaps also in coastal areas of Gascony (Les Landes), where, as in Basque and Spanish, a three rather than a four opening vowel system system is used.[7]

Other Perspectives

We will now describe ideas proposed by various researchers, particularly by linguists, with the intention of situating the Basques in a wider European context.

---

7. The f > h transformation in Spanish is a characteristic whose origin some explain as the influence of Basque on Romance when the court of the early kings of Castile was still bilingual. This would also explain the unusual creation of dipthongs in Spanish from Romance (ɔɛ) in the tonic position (*mortem* (death) becomes *muerte*; *perdit* (he/she loses), *pierde*), a type of adaptation from a system with four degrees of opening (Romance) to one that only has three (Basque).

Following Ramón de Abadal's research (*Els comtats de Pallars i Ribagorça*, The counties of Pallars and Ribagorça, Barcelona, 1955), Joan Corominas who, among other subjects, has researched Pyrenean toponymy, has suggested that an astonishing number of village names in the High Pyrenees, between Navarre and Andorra, are Basque in origin, and he bases this idea on solid linguistic foundation (*La toponymie hispanique préromane et la survivance du basque jusqu'au bas Moyen Age*, Pre-Roman Hispanic toponymy and the survival of Basque to the Middle Ages, 1960): the Upper Aragón Valley (47), Sobrarbe (151), the Upper Ribagorza (30), and the Upper Pallars (90). The unusual phonetics in the forms of Roman origin and the great number of names that can credibly be argued to have Basque origins have led him to conclude that these valleys used to be Basque-speaking and that the ancestral language survived, along with Romance, until a very late date, perhaps up until the eighth century. This thesis is supported by Spanish archaeologist L. Pericot Garcia, who believes that, during the protohistorical periods, the whole of the Pyrenees, with Catalonia and the Basque Country as its two focus points, were inhabited by livestock farming peoples whose ethnological characteristics were identical to those of the proto-Basques.

Johannes Hubschmid (*Mediterrane Substrate*, Mediterranean substrata, 1960) takes lexical considerations and suffixes into accout to demonstrate that Basque has features from two different non Indo-European linguistic strata that the languages around the Mediterranean have borrowed from.

First, a Euro-African stratum, the oldest in the west, which has long been understood as the Hispanic-Caucasian stratum. Very old migrations during the prehistorical or protohistorical periods explain these exchanges that, in fact, are not restricted to the Mediterranean, with the author also linking them to Finnish, Estonian, and Burushaski, a language isolate spoken in northern Pamir, not to mention contacts with Indo-Europeans. This wide-reaching thesis, which is often convincing and reminds one of the vast perspectives opened up by L. Pericot Garcia, proposes the idea of multiple, thousand-year-old and unsuspected relationships between Europe and neighboring regions in Asia and Africa and tries to prove that Basque, far from being a language isolate, has in fact been a part of massive cultural movements—in the widest sense of the term—which have affected this part of the world.

Today, certain linguists who have studied Basque, such as G. Dumézil and R. Lafon, defend the existence of a kinship that, at first sight, seems very surprising, between Basque and the Caucasian languages. These languages, of which Georgian is the best known at present, are nowadays as isolated as Basque and are divided up on the slope of a mountain range twice the size of the Pyrenees. There is such variety between the various different languages that their original unity is no more than a matter of conjecture. Many of them are scarcely known, and have only recently been studied, which makes it more difficult to compare them with a language–Basque–whose oldest surviving texts, let us not forget, date from the sixteenth century.

In the absence of any "Common Caucasian," comparisons have to be made with the vocabulary and grammatical system of each language in order to find any similarity with Basque language features. It seems reasonable to accept that there are a considerable number of lexical similarities, but, above all, it is the "multipersonal" nature of the verbs and their ergative construction (to be found in Northeastern Caucasian languages and, in some morphosyntactical cases, in Georgian) that make it possible to suggest a Basque-Caucasian kinship as a thesis. All verbs in Georgian, for instance, have forms similar to the Basque "synthetic" verbs, with morphemes stating the various different participants in each action or state: subject, object, recipient, and so on.

Are these remains from far-distant contacts, migrations, a difficult to prove Basque-Caucasian unity dating from before the Indo-European invasions? With our current knowledge, it is not possible to make any decisive statement about this (see Hubschimid's theories). Nevertheless, archaeology also points to similarities between Caucasian and Pyrenean cultures and studies of blood types (which we will examine below) also provide evidence that favors this possible kinship.[8]

In this research into the origins of the Basques, we are going to make use of a relatively recent science that is gaining in strength: studies of blood types.

Hirszfeld and Hirszfeld were the first to demonstrate, around 1917–1919, that the frequency of blood groups varies from people to people. With regard to Western Europe, and in general with white-skinned people, the Basques are unusual, as A. E. Mourant, Moulinier, and J. Ruffié have demonstrated. A very high number of Basques have blood type O, few have blood type A, and almost none blood type B. With regard to the Rh blood group system, they are even more unusual in that they have the greatest known frequency of Rh- in the world.

These blood group characterisics overflow, progressively, into the current Basque language pool and are clearly to be found in what A.-V. Vallois calls the "southwestern corner of France" and what is the "Aquitaine perimeter." Recently J. Ruffié and J. Bernard[9] have observed that there are close connections among blood relatives with a high frequency of blood group O and Rh- and certain linguistic, toponymic, and cultural traits: this points to the existence of an ancient Basque culture and language beyond its current boundaries.

While the language has been lost outside the current Basque provinces (possibly since the late Middle Ages), biologically the inhabitants have retained their ancestral characteristics. They are certainly descended from the people who inhabited Europe before the Bronze Age and who were driven toward the Southwest France

---

8. Let us remember a strange fact. While the Iberians of Spain seem to have been related to the Basques in some very remote way, authors in antiquity (cf. Valerius Flaccus, *Argonautica*, 6, 120) also called part of the Caucasus, what is today Georgia, *Iberia*. Likewise, the word "Iberian" is used to describe Christian literature in contemporary Georgia.

9. Jacques Ruffié and Jean Bernard, "Peuplement du Sud-Ouest Européen. Les relations entre la biologie et la culture," *Cahiers d'Anthropologie et d'Ecologie humaine* 2, no. 2 (1974), pp. 3–18.

by groups of Indo-Europeans who came from the East and brought different languages and civilizations with them.

Only the reduced area in the Western Pyrenees and, to an extent, the neighboring regions have retained any trace of the original culture. It was these old inhabitants, with their Rh-, who lived in much of Europe.

These observations confirm and give precision to Bosch-Gimpers's hypothesis that the Basques, who are different from other inhabitants of the Pyrenees in terms of osteology, are the oldest group in the mountain range.

3

Historical Events

While, in general, the Basque Country's "marginal" position with regard to great events means that there is little information about its history, its proximity to Castile has made it of greater interest to historians to the south of the Pyrenees than to those to the north: the destiny of France was decided far from the Basque Country.

From the Romans to the Migration Period

It is well known that Rome was interested in the Peninsula long before it was in Gaul, but it was never able to entirely control the fiercely independent inhabitants of the Pyrenees.

During the Republic, Cato was sent to Spain to pacify a country in revolt and reached *Iacca* (Jaca) in 194 BCE. Fifteen years later, Tiberius Sempronius Gracchus, given the same mission, stabilized the situation and founded *Gracc(h)ur(r)is* to replace native Ilurcis.

After the Celiberians were crushed (133 BCE, the siege of Numancia), Spain became the theater of war for the rivalry between Pompey and Sertorius, the "democrat"; when the former won he founded *Pompaelo*, calling it after himself, in 75 BCE. Two years later the latter, fleeing from the man who had defeated him, took refuge in Osca (Huesca), where he had founded a school, and it was there that he was killed. That city, along with Calagurris (where all the inhabitants killed themselves), was one of the last to resist Pompey, while the Basques, who had been on the losing side, regrouped on the banks of the Garonne and founded *Urbs*

Convenarum (the future Saint-Bertrand-de-Comminges) there: the "town of fugitives."

During Caesar's campaigns in Gaul, it was his lieutenant Crassus who subjected the people of Aquitaine in 56 BCE. The Basques had come from the other side of the Pyrenees to help them. Over there, Caesar himself defeated Pompey's troops at *Ilerda* (Lleida), thus controlling the whole of Hispania Citerior.

In turn, Augustus sent his legate Statilius Taurus, whose victory over the Cantabri, the Asturs, and the Vaccaei was scarcely enough to control the restless mountain people. It would be Agrippa, ten years later, who established a lasting peace that was maintained until the Migration Period. As far as Aquitaine was concerned, Crassus's victory was not enough to pacify it and both Agrippa (from 39 to 38 BCE) and Corvinus Messala (from 28 to 27 BCE) had to intervene at later dates.

Augustus's iniciative to join Caesar's Aquitaine with the Celtic peoples between the Loire and the Garonne seems to have made the former peoples create their own separate unity, *Novempopulanie*, of the "country of nine people,"[1] whose capital was Éauze (*Elusa*); this rupture is illustrated and consecrated by the famous Gallo-Roman inscription in Hazparne.

---

1. In fact, more than nine have been counted: Pliny (Natural History, 4, 29, 1) numbers twenty-eight! A dozen of them can be situated with almost complete certainty: from north to south, the Boiates (Pays de Buch, near Arcachon), the Vasates (Bazas, ancient Cossio), the Cocosates (Les Landes, near Sescouze), the Sotiates (Sos, Lot-et-Garonne), the Alusates (Éauze, Gers), the Lactorates (Lectoure, Gers), the Ausci (Auch, Gers), the Tarbelli (the Atlantic coast and the Aturri basin: not Tarbes!), the Vanarni (Béarn, cf. Beneharnum Lescar), the Begarri (Bigorre, around Saint-Lezer), the Lasunni, the Upper Pau Valley, cf. Saint-Hilaire-de-*Lassun*), the Onobrisates (Upper Aturri Valley, cf. Cieutat-de-*Neurest*, the old name for Cieutat), the Onessi (the Pique Valley, around Luchon), the Consoranni (Gascon Ariege or Couserans, around Saint-Lizier, ancient Lugdunum Consorannorum). There is less certainly about situating the Camponi (Kanbo, Pyrenees-Atlantiques or Campan, Hautes-Pyrenees?), the Pimpedunni (a Celtic name meaning "the five towns", cf. Bortziriak (the Five Towns) in the Bidasoa Valley), the Sibyllates (Zuberoa, *vallis Subola* during the Middle Ages), to mention just the least doubtful ones. See H. Delbreilh, "L'Aquitaine préromaine," research paper, unpublished, Toulouse-Le Miraile University (Professor M. Larousse).

From the Migration Period to the End of the Visigoth Kingdom of Spain

Pax romana seems to have ruled over a land in which the only migrations were internal (the *Vascones* toward the west, who pushed the Varduli toward the Autrigones, farther to the west) until the start of the Migration Period.

While the Vandals and the Suebi crossed the land without stopping, in 413 CE the Visigoths occupied all the the Gallo-Romano lands to the south of the Loire and also Gallia Narbonensis as far as the Alps, making Toulouse their capital five years later. It was the most powerful kingdom in Western Europe at that time. However, Clovis's Franks defeated them at Vouillé in 541, taking Pamplona-Iruñea and besieging Zaragoza, and the Visigoths emmigrated to Spain en masse, choosing Toledo as their new capital.

The Franks, from the north and the Visigoths, from the south, continually intervened in the western Pyrenees to put down uprisings.[2] The Merovingians managed to impose a duke in ancient Novempopulania, but this Duke of Vasconia—the new name of the Aquitainian triangle, which was later to become Gascony—inherited his people's "vocation for independence," which was seldom given up until the times of Henry IV.

---

2. There is no sound basis to Oihenart's opinion (*Notitiae utriusque Vasconiae*), which is still widely accepted today, that the current population of the French Basque Country is derived from an invasion of Vascones from the other side of the Pyrenees toward the end of the sixth century who occupied an area that had been as thoroughly Romanized as the rest of Gascony. Basque toponomy reveals no sign of that supposed Romanization and because it is known that a single term—Vascones—was often used in medieval Latin to talk about both the Basques and the Gascons (the former also being called Bascli), historical sources from the Middle Ages can give us no definitive assurances on this matter. On the contrary, offering hypotheses is extremely difficult and we limit them to the Basques north of the Pyrenees: G. Rohlfs, R. Lafon, and so on, believe that these descendants of the Aquitainians had escaped Romanization, having been far from the centers of Gallo-Roman culture until the present day, abandoned their ancestral language and replaced it directly with French. As regards the name Vasconia (Gascony) being taken on by Novempopulania, that only reflects a re-Basquifying of the whole land and is not similar to the term *Vascongada* (Basquified), used to describe the Spanish provinces of Gipuzkoa, Bizkaia, and Araba, where Basque has always been spoken.

The reader must consult specialist works for later information about Gascony. Despite the names of some of the first dukes (Aznar, Gartzea/García, Antso/Sancho), they were Romanized, at least on the plains.[3] It must also be said that the scarcity of documents makes the history of Gascony from the eighth to the tenth century a "challenge for historians" as F. Lot put it. Thus, on the French side, from now on we will limit ourselves to examining the Basque Country as it is currently defined. To return to that period, in the western area the Visigoths, from the times of Reccared up to the last kings, Wamba, Wittiza, and Rodrigo, repressed Basque uprisings continually. But their kingdom was toppled at the battle of Guadalete (711) at which the Arabs, who had landed at Gibraltar and were commanded by Tariq, were victorious.

The Beginnings of the Kingdom of Navarre

The following year the Islamic armies reached as far as northern Aragón. Meanwhile, the kings of Asturias tried to rally all the forces under their banner to open a path southward and the Basques of Pamplona-Iruñea, having removed the Moor Mutarrif from their government and replaced him with a certain Velasco (799), slowly became an autonomous center of resistance that other nuclei from the north of the Pyrenees joined.[4] The first, semi-legendary king of Pamplona-Iruñea, Eneko Aritza [Íñigo Arista in Spanish] (840–

---

3. Things certainly did not change as quickly in the Pyrenean valleys (cf. J. Coromin's thesis, p. 20): the first King of Navarre's family was from Bigorre and verse 384 of the *Chanson de sainte Foy* [Song of Saint Foy], one of the first texts in Occitan literature (tenth century), also points in the same direction: *Cisclaun* l *Bascon qe son d'Aran*, translated by P. Alfaric and E. Hoepffner: "The Basques from the Aran valley scream," which they sound ill at ease with. In fact, these Bascons, in contrast to the Gascons, are indeed "Basques" and it should be remembered that the toponym Aran comes from the Basque *aran* (valley).

4. These were the celebrated Basques who, in 778, famously ambushed Charlemagne at Orreaga (Roncevaux in French, Roncesvalles in Spanish) and annihilated his rearguard and its commander, Roland. Some fifty years later, in 824, a similar misfortune, though less deadly, befell the Frankish Counts Ebles and Aznar, who Louis the Pious had sent, accompanied by troops, to Pamplona-Iruñea.

859?), who was originally from Bigorre,[5] kept a policy of independence, occasionally allying with Islamic forces against others, and only accepting dependence on the Kingdom of Asturias in a very loose sense.

A second Navarrese dynasty, the Ximena [Jimena] family, came to rule in Pamplona-Iruñea in 905, the first of its three sovereigns being Antso Gartzez [Sancho Garcés in Spanish]. With the Count of Aragón as a dependant from 922 onward, the King of Navarre allied with the Kingdom of Asturias-León in 937 to fight against Abd al-Rahman III, who had pillaged and burned Pamplona-Iruñea. The famous battle of Simancas, two years later, consolidated this successful coalition of all the Hispanic kingdoms of the northwest, from Galicia to Castile and including the mountain-dwelling Basques, against the Islamic forces of Cordoba and Zaragoza.

It was then that Castile was born, on the old land of the Autrigones that had become Vardulia, "a confluence of races, roads, and frontiers," as the historian Sánchez Albornoz puts it, growing up by combining, in the heat of the Reconquest, the genes of the Celts, the Iberians, and the Basques. The province of Castile, which had possessed *free rights* since the eighth century, started, in the tenth century and under Count Fernán González, to have a resolute policy of independence from the Kingdom of León. It is no idle dream to imagine the legendary Navarrese pride playing a decisive part in the very genes of Castile, which was to fulfill a prestigious destiny. Be that as it may, the small province became a kingdom in 1036, increasingly becoming a powerful center of attraction for neighboring states in its competition with Navarre.

Navarre from the Reign of Antso III Gartzez (or the Great) to the House of Champagne

Son of Antso II Gartzez Abarka [Sancho Garcés II "Abarca" in Spanish], the third king of the Ximena dynasty, Antso III Gartzez

---

5. Was Bigorre still Basque-speaking at that time? This cannot be excluded if we bear in mind what we have said above about the Aran Valley, which is farther east and, so, in principle, less resistant to Romanization.

[Sancho Garcés III in Spanish] (1000–1035) managed to make his kingdom prestigious enough to attract most of the smaller states, which won him the nickname the Great ["Nagusia" in Basque, "el Mayor" in Spanish]. The Dukes of Gascony were vassals of his; Lapurdi and Lower Navarre paid homage to him; he annexed Bizkaia and Araba thanks to his marriage. Outside the Basque territory, he also took the Pyrenean lands of Sobrabe, Ribagorza, and Pallars into his kingdom; to the east, the Count of Aragón was already subject to the Kingdom of Navarre, his grandfather, Gartzea I [García Sánchez I in Spanish], having married one of the daughters of the family. Lastly, because the first Vicounts of Zuberoa were subject to the Dukes of Gascony, they, too, were indirectly subject to the King of Navarre, suzerain of the Dukes of Gascony.

Antso the Great's successor, his son Gartzea III [García Sánchez III in Spanish] "of Najera," had to fight against his own brother Fernando, who had become the first king of Castile, in 1054 at the battle of Atapuerca, in which he died.

His son, Antso IV [Sancho Garcés IV in Spanish] "of Peñalen," in turn had to fight against Sancho Fernández, prince of Castile, son of Alfonso IV, and with his cousin Sancho Ramírez of Aragón. The latter was the victor of the "War of the Three Sanchos,"[6] but peace favored Castile. The King of Navarre was murdered in 1074 at Peñalon, which is the derivation of his nickname.

The last quarter of the eleventh century is rich in events of great historical importance. Antso of Peñalen's throne passed to the kings of Aragón Sancho [Ramírez] (1074–1094), Pedro I (1094–1104) and, finally, Alfonso the Battler (1104–1134), while, at the same time, the king of neighboring Castile, Alfonso IV (1072–1109), who had succeeded Ferdinand I, took control of the county of Araba.

This latter king, who took the title Emperor of León and Castile, and later on *Imperator totius Hispaniae*, was victorious against the Moors, whose small kingdoms in the south of the

6. Translator's Note: Antso is translated as Sancho in Spanish.

peninsula (the *taifas*) were driven to seek the assistance of the Almoravids in Africa, which led to the second Arab invasion of Spain (1086). When Alfonso lost the battle of Fraga, dying without descendants, the people of Navarre chose a new king, Gartzia V [García Ramírez in Spanish] the Restorer (1134–1150). Gartzia V soon named Ladrón de Guevara Count of Gipuzkoa (1135), perhaps trying to take measures against Castile to which the province, which had been separated from it in 1076, was once more subject twelve years later.

Alfonso VII, King of Castile from 1126, made Navarre and Aragón his protectorates. Antso VI [Sancho VI in Spanish], the Wise, succeeded to the throne of Pamplona-Iruñea, and during his reign numerous events took place in the neighboring kingdoms. In Aragón, Alfonso II (1162–1196) linked the destiny of his country with that of Catalonia due to inheritance.

In Castile, Alfonso VIII came to the throne in 1166 of a state that had been reduced to half of what it had been under his predecessor, Sancho III of Castile, who had divided the kingdom between his two sons. For some time Alfonso fought against his uncle, the King of Navarre, who had picked quarrels with him during his minority, and then made peace with him (Fitero, 1177). He then managed to obtain Gipuzkoa for his kingdom, annexing it in 1200, and then Araba, taking Vitoria-Gasteiz in 1200 with the aid of the Bizkaian López de Haro, while the Gipuzkoans, who had at first seemed hesitant (it was Antso VI of Navarre who had granted Donostia-San Sebastián its charter in 1180), finally came to support the Kingdom of Castile. This gatherer of lands also inherited the Duchy of Gascony through his marriage to Eleanor, the daughter of Henry II of England, although he had to take the duchy by force.

During the last years of the century, two thrones were taken by new rulers: in Navarre, Antso VII [Sancho VII in Spanish] the Strong (1194) and, two years later, in Aragón-Catalonia, Pedro II. The former died in 1234. During his reign, Lower Navarre (in other words, the old fiefdoms of Arberoa [Arberoue], Oztibarre

[Ostabarret], Ortzaize [Ossès], Uharte-Garazi [Uhart-Cize], Amikuze [Pays de Mixe], and Baigorri) had been annexed to the crown
of Pamplona-Iruñea as an external county (*Merindad de Ultra-
Puertos*). On his death, a dynasty from Champagne came to the
throne.

Pedro II was killed at the Battle of Muret in 1213, where he
had been allied with the Occitan lords against the Crusaders (the
Albigensinian or Cathar Crusade). The previous year he had
been wounded at the no less well-known Battle of Las Navas of
Tolosa (in the province of Jaen, Andalusia), in which the allied
Castilian, Navarrese, and Aragonese armies defeated the Almo-
had troops.[7]

In Navarre, when Antso [Sancho in Spanish] the Strong died
(1234), he was succeeded by his nephew the young count Theobald
of Champagne (our troubadour!) in spite of his old uncle's plots
against him in association with Jaime I of Aragón (Treaty of
Tutera, 1231). After Theobald II (1253–1270) and Henry (1270–
1274), Joan I succeeded to the throne and, in 1284, married Philip
IV the Fair of France to benefit from his protection.

Three Kings of France and Navarre followed: Louis X the
Quarreler (1307–1316), Philip V the Tall (1316–1322), and Charles
IV the Fair (1322–1327). But the people of Navarre did not accept
the candidature of Philip VI of Valois, and, in 1328, the crown
passed to the House of Évreux whose heir, Count Philip, was married to Joan II, daughter of Louis the Quarreler. Their dynasty did
not start under very favorable auspices, in that they were immediately called on to fight against the Castilians, who had invaded
and chased them from Gipuzkoa and later defeated them at Tutera
(1335).

---

7. The Almohads had arrived in 1146 to support and reinforce the Almoravids.
The chains on the shield of Navarre (which were not on its original coat of arms)
are believed to represent those which the Navarrese troops took from the Arab camp
that day, from around Miramamolin (Abu abd Allah Muhammad al-Nasir)'s tent, to
forge the railings around the Pamplona-Iruñea cathedral.

The Northern Provinces up to the Period of English Domination

Stemming from three Gallo-Roman *pagi*, at the start of the feudal era each had a specific statute. To the east, the Viscounty of Zuberoa was subject at first to the Dukes of Gascony and the Counts of Bigorre and later, from 1078, to the Viscounts of Béarn. In the center, the fiefdoms of Arberoa, Oztibarre, Ortzaize, Amikuze, Uharte-Garazi, and Baigorri, which are documented from the start of the eleventh century, were to become an external county (*Merindad de Ultra-Puertos*) two hundred years later, an integral part of the Kingdom of Navarre until 1530. The Viscounty of Lapurdi, finally, initally subject to Antso the Great of Navarre, became subject to the Dukes of Gascony in 1033.

All of these lands were allodial and enjoyed particular liberties, being free from any servitude. When the Kings of England became the Dukes of Gascony by marriage (1155), Eleanor of Aquitaine taking Henry II of England (Henry Plantagenet) as her second husband, they obliged the Viscounts and Barons of Zuberoa and Lapurdi to give up their rights in public matters, in this way suppressing their feudal rights, in contrast with Lower Navarre. Social hierarchies there were already linked to the statute of each "house," known, from the bottom to the top of the scale, as *fivatière*, *franche*, *infançonne*, and *noble*.

However, the local nobility took poorly to English domination, which led to Richard the Lionheart [Richard I of England] sieging and taking Baiona. In 1204, King Alfonso VIII of Castile, who had inherited the Duchy of Gascony by marrying Henry Plantagenet's daughter Eleanor, invaded Zuberoa and Lapurdi and burned Baiona to the ground in order to take effective charge of the duchy.

In Zuberoa, Viscount Auger de Miramont also rebelled against the English, but Philip the Fair obliged him to make his lands subject to Louis the Quarreler, King of Navarre, who then gave them back to him. These feudal rebellions (which resulted in the appointment of a bailiff of Lapurdi in 1245, responsible for keeping direct contact open between the sovereign and the people) led to the people having closer relationships with the English, and often being against France.

From the Champagne Dynasty in Navarre to the French Revolution

The Southern Provinces: The Annexation of Navarre to the Crown of Castile

After Charles the Bad, who succeeded Joan II of Navarre, Charles III the Noble came to the throne (1387-1425) and surrounded himself with French people who, among other things, were responsible for building the palace of Erriberri.

His daughter Blanche I, who succeeded him, maried Don Juan, Count of Peñafiel, and gave him a son, Charles, Prince of Viana, around whom a faction of the Navarrese nobility rallied, led by the Count of Lerin, the Baron of Lüküze [Luxe] (in Amikuze), and Louis de Beaumont (the "Beaumontais"). The other faction of the nobility followed the banner of the Count of Gramont and favored Don Juan (the "Agramontais").[8]

When Charles was finally toppled and fled to Naples, Don Juan, alias John II, accepted that he would be succeeded by his youngest daughter Eleanor, who was married to Gaston de Foix. In the Treaty of Baiona (1462), Louis XI of France agreed to help John in exchange for Roussillon and Sardinia.

When John II died in 1479, Eleanor inherited the throne of Navarre, but she immediately abdicated in favor of her son Francis Phoebus. His sister Catherine married Jean d'Albret in 1484, which may have made the Castilians fear that Navarre would eventually fall to the Crown of France. Ferdinand the Catholic of Spain prevented this from happening by invading; Catherine and Jean fled to France (1512).

---

8. One bloody episode of this rivalry is portrayed in Berterretch's celebrated Zuberoan lament.

The situation was clarified definitively when Charles V, Holy Roman Emperor, separated the two halves of Navarre, evacuating Lower Navarre while Upper Navarre, to the south of the Pyrenees, became attached to the Kingdom of Castile.

The Northern Provinces, from the French Conquest to the Treaty of the Pyrenees

It was not until the mid-fifteenth century that English domination ceased in Southwest France. Baiona did not fall until 1451, after Gaston Phoebus [Gaston III, Count of Foix] took the castles at Gixune [Guiche], in Lapurdi, and Maule, in Zuberoa.

Zuberoa became subject to the French Crown in 1510. This province, because of its proximity to Béarn (Jean d'Albret's land), was the first to be affected by the Protestant Reformation. Lower Navarre soon followed.[9] The bloody troubles that marked this period only finished when Jean d'Albret died (1572).

Later, after having been sadly illustrated by the witch trails that Pierre de Lancre, a judge from Bordeaux, directed from 1608 onward, it was under prestigious auspices that Lapurdi became the focus of attention for France and the whole of Europe fifty years later. It was then, in 1659, that Mazarin and Don Luis de Haro signed the famous Treaty of the Pyrenees on Pheasant Island in Hendaia. The following year, Louis XIV married the Spanish princess Maria Teresa.[10] Perhaps it was inspired by this "raft" of events that Vauban transformed the fortifications at Baiona shortly afterward, finished those at Sokoa, near Donibane Lohizune, and those at Hendaia, and improved those at Donibane Garazi.

As the maritime activity of the people of Donibane Lohizune diminished after the whales disappeared and cod became scarcer, the energy and hardiness of the people of Lapurdi found an outlet as privateers at the service of the king. Among others, Duconte, Harismendy, Saint-Martin, Dolabaratz, Larregui, Haramboure,

---

9. It was the Lower Navarrese Joanes Leizarraga from Beskoitze who translated the (reformed) Bible into Basque for the first time (1571).

10. Translator's Note: They married at Donibane Lohizune, also in Lapurdi.

and Etcheverry were all privateers, as was the famous "Svigaray-chipi dit Croisic, capitaine de frégate du roy,"[11] whose tombstone can still be seen in the old wooden church in Placentia, the old French capital of the island of Newfoundland.

Sociopolitical Structure and Institutions in the Basque Country

On the eve of the French Revolution, the Basque provinces both north and south of the Pyrenees were relatively homogenous in these respects:

The population, which was completely free, was divided into classes depending on property wealth and, in the upper echelons, on titles of nobility;

Authority was wealded by elected people and controlled by popular assemblies that met on a regular basis;

Freedom was guaranteed by written laws (*foruak* [Basque], *fors* [French], or *fueros* [Spanish]: the old laws or charters) designed to protect individuals and diverse social groups both against the mis-use of central power, held by "royal officers'," and against other groups or individuals from society's infringements;

Local assemblies controlled how these laws were applied in practical terms and also set their own budgets, while also taking part, occasionally, in the matter of royal taxes.

However, this general profile varied in the different provinces, and 'the history of each province meant that age-old tradition influenced each one considerably.

In Araba, the upper classes consisted of non-titled nobility (*hidalgos*) and the clergy. The more modest classes were made up of employed workers, others who were partially self-employed (*colla-zos*) and, lastly, of those who were orginally serfs to the nobility and the clergy (these latter were emancipated in the twelfth century, which is when the charters were drawn up: the charter of Vitoria-Gasteiz, in 1181, the charter of Guardia in 1168, and so on).

---

11. "Svigaraychipi known as Croisic, the King's frigate captain."

Local urban and rural areas sent representatives to General Assemblies (*Batzar Nagusiak* [Basque], *Juntas Generales* [Spanish]) twice a year. A commission, consisting of two commissioners and four representatives, made sure that the decisions taken were carried out. The foral veto (*foru pase, pase foral*) made it possible to check that royal orders did not contradict the terms of the charters.

The social and geographical structure of Bizkaia was complex. The province was divided into the "plains" (*tierra llana*) or countryside and the *villas* or towns,[12] and two specific areas: the district of Durango (*Durangaldea/Duranguesado*) and Enkarterri/Encartaciones, the most westerly part of the province, to the west of the Nerbioi River. The seigniory of Bizkaia was subject to Castile from 1370 onward: the king was represented by a royal representive (the *corregidor*) and his lieutenants.

The *villas* and the *tierra llana* sent their representatives to the General Assemblies (*Batzar Nagusiak/Juntas Generales*), which met every two years; initially, in Idoibaltzaga[13] and, from the fifteenth century onward, in Gernika, the meetings being held under the famous oak tree there; those from the district of Durango met in Gerediaga; those from Enkarterri met in Avellaneda. The *tierra llana* was governed according to custom, the towns by statutes and charters granted by nobles. The people of Bizkaia did not pay tributes to Castile, but they were obliged to carry out military service.

Gipuzkoa, originally a *behetria*,[14] was subject to the kings of Navarre and Castile. At first the royal representative was called the *adelantado* and, later on, the *corregidor*. The people were divided into three groups: the untitled nobility (*hidalgos*) in the *villas*; the employed workers; and the *parientes mayores*.[15]

---

12. These towns had certain priviledges that villages did not.

13. Translator's Note: Now known as Errigoiti (Rigoitia, Bizkaia).

14. A territory in which the inhabitants were free to choose their own lord.

15. Landed nobility.

The *villas*, protected by *fueros*, formed associations to counter-balance the power of the *parientes mayores*, and these associations joined together in the fifteenth century as a general association that, from then on, organized General Assemblies (*Batzar Nagusiak/Juntas Generales*) twice a year in the different towns. The votes were proportional to the "hearths" (households) in each *concejo* (municipality). As in Araba, the foral veto guaranteed that the decisions taken were in line with the *fueros*.[16]

Navarre was divided into five *merindades* (districts): *Ultra Puertos* (Lower Navarre), Pamplona-Iruñea, Lizarra, Zangoza [Sangüesa], and Tutera, with that of Erriberri being added in 1407. For the period, it was a model state organization.

The population (which reached 105,000 in the fifteenth century) initially included *francos* (foreigners), Mudejar or Moorish people (Muslims), and Jews, as well as the native Basques. The nobility (which was of Basque origin, like the clergy), was divided into *fijosdalgos* (*hidalgos* or *infanzones,* untitled nobility)[17] and *ricoshombres* (literally "rich men," meaning titled nobility).

The whole of society, divided into three branches (ecclesiatical, noble, and of the people), was represented at the Cortes (parliament) of Navarre, an assembly that dates from the thirteenth century and that gave rise, in the fifteenth century, to the royal council (in charge of legal matters) and the provincial council (in charge

---

16. These three provinces were to the setting of a bloody rivalry between family lineages. There were twenty-four of these in Gipuzkoa, fifteen supporting the house of Oñaz (the Oñacinos) and nine the house of Gamboa (the Gamboinos); the burning of Arrasate [Mondragón] by the latter was the subject of a famous Basque epic song. In Araba, the Ayalas fought against the Callejas, the house of Haro against that of Treviño. In Bizkaia, the Urquizu and Abendaño faction opposed the Muxicas and the Buitrons, and so on. It was also in the fifteenth century that the Agramontais and the Beaumontais fought each other. But the Basques have always been hot blooded: two centuries later, the *sabel xuri* (white bellies) and *sabel gorri* (red bellies) killed each other in Lapurdi after one of Louis XIV's act of authority favored the Urtubies over the Caupennes, who were backed by the notary of Azkaine [Ascain], Martin Chourio.

17. Those named by the king to form part of the nobility were titled *infançones de abarca* (*abarca* meaning sandal).

of fiscal and economic affairs). A century later, the chamber of accounts was also founded.

Finance (which was administered in a way closer to the French model than that of Aragón or Castile) was raised from four sources: royal rights, feudal rights, *alcabalas* (taxes raised on sales), and *cuarteles* (exceptional taxes voted by the parliament). Jews and Muslims were subject to a special tax system. The *fuero general* (general charter)[18] to which the kingdom was subject was decreed in 1330.

However, Lower Navarre had its own leglistative body, made up of delgates from the five *villes* or towns (Donapaleu, Donibane Garazi, Bastida, Garrüze [Garris], and Larzabale [Larceveau]), and there were also representatives from Uharte-Garazi, Baigorri, Ortzaize, Amikuze, Arberoa, and Oztibarre in first level local assemblies. These assemblies had their own recognized prerogatives: they took charge of all civil administration, ensuring the province's financial autonomy and guaranteeing that the *for* or charter was respected (cf. the foral veto on the other side of the Pyrenees).

With regard to this *for*, the *fuero general* remained in force in the district of *Ultra Puertos* until 1608; but, in 1611, Louis XIII imposed a new *for* (which was written in the Béarnais dialect of Gascon).

The institutions of Lapurdi were a fine example of democratic simplicity. The masters of "free houses" (in which local chamber assemblies met every Sunday in each parish to administer small local matters) were chosen by *jurats* (boards or panels) every year, with one of them acting as mayor. All the mayors met in Uztaritze, when general meetings were called, to make up the provincial assembly or *Bilçar* (*Biltzarra* in contemporary Basque), which included neither the nobility nor the clergy!

The *Biltzarra*'s prerogatives, like those of the Cour d'Ordre (court of order or general council) in Zuberoa, are comparable to those of the Lower Navarrese council. Royal authority in the province was represented by a bailiff and a "general lieutenant," as well

18. Written in Navarrese-Aragonese, not Basque.

as the king's prosecutor. The traditional laws (*lege zaharrak*) were organized, written down, and printed by Louis XII and François I in 1553.

Finally, Zuberoa was administered in a less systematic way and under a highly complex structure:[19] The provincial assembly was known as the court of order and it met twice a year at the same time as two other bodies, the *Assemblée du Grand Corps* (made up of nobles and the clergy), which met in Litxarre [Licharre], near Maule,[20] and the *Silviet*, a popular assembly similar to the *Biltzarra* in Lapurdi, which met in Irabarne [Libarrenx]. The latter body was dissolved in 1730. The laws of Zuberoa were written down and published at the same time as those of Lapurdi.

From the French Revolution until Today

At the close of the eighteenth century in France and during the first three quarters of the nineteenth century in Spain both traditional and liberal (and often democratic) political and social structures disappeared; structures that the Basques had formed over the centuries to marry their way of being with the old land where they had always lived. The centralizing Jacobin power that has dominated Europe for the last two centuries had condemned them. In France, the Basques were unable to resist the changes brought about by the Revolution; in Spain, they linked their destiny with that of a family and a faction and did not survive its defeat.

The Southern Provinces: Carlism, the Abolition of the Fueros, World Wars, and the Civil War

The Age of Enlightenment, without finishing in cataclysm as it did in France, did lead to "enlightened" initiatives in the Southern

---

19. There were three independent administrative areas: the town (*ville*) of Maule, six royal boroughs (Barkoxe [Barcus], Montori, Atharratze, Hauze [Haux], Santa Grazi, and Larraine [Larrau]) and, lastly, three *messageries*, divided into seven *dégairies*, which covered all the remaining parishes in Zuberoa.

20. The name Litxarre seems to be derived from **ili zaharra* (the old town); it is the old town opposite the castle and on the other bank of the Ühaitza River.

Basque Country that, in the second half of the century, saw the creation of "economic societies." The first, and the most important, was the Sociedad Vascongada de los Amigos del País (The Basque Society of Friends of the Country), which the Count of Pañaflorida founded in 1765 in order to increase the prosperity and well-being of the Basque Country[21] by encouraging the use of applied sciences. Later it set up the Real Seminario Partriótico Vasco (Royal Basque Patriotic School) in the Jesuits' old college in Bergara, after the latter had been expelled, and was open during the last years of the century.

Carlism was the big issue during the following century in the Basque Country. In addition to problems of dynastic succession, it was a chance to use arms to claim and defend the Basques' dual ancestral priviledge, which was under threat: respect for traditional freedom (which was guaranteed by the *fueros*) domestically, and the relative political independence of the Basque provinces from Madrid.[22]

The king of Spain, Charles IV of the House of Bourbon, great grandson of Louis XIV, had two sons, Fernando and Carlos ("Don Carlos"). The former succeeded his father in 1808 under the title Fernando VII, although Napolean removed him from the throne, to which he did not return until 1813. Until 1823 he carried out anti-liberal policies. He revoked the Spanish Salic Law[23] and made his daughter heiress to the crown under the name Isabel II, at the expense of his own brother, Carlos.

When Fernando died in 1833, Carlos, disinherited, fled to Portugal accompanied by his wife, Maria Francisca, and her sister, Maria Teresa, princess of Beira, who supported him. He went on to London where, encouraged by the two princesses and by Gen-

---

21. This initiative was limited in scope to the three *Vascongadas* provinces as can be seen on the society's emblem: three hands with entwined fingers under the motto *Irurac Bat* (The Three (Provinces) Are as One).

22. Research is currenly being done into sociological support for Carlism; we do not yet have the conclusions.

23. This law had been promulgated by Phillip V in 1713 to avoid Spain and France ever being ruled by the same monarch.

eral Zumalacárregui, he prepared to return to Spain. In October he proclaimed himself king of Spain and started a war that was to last seven years and would be fought in the southern Basque provinces and in the neighboring lands to the south (the *Maestrazgo*).

At first, the adversaries observed each other, fortified their positions and raided each other's territory. Then Zumalacárregui died of wounds during the first siege of Bilbao and was replaced by General Maroto. The next phase of the war, which was to last two years, started with large-scale military initiatives launched by the Carlist captain general, Don Sebastian, son of the princess of Beira, whom Don Carlos, a widower since Maria Francisca had died in 1834, married four years later.

However, although the Carlist army got as far as Madrid at once in 1837, it was demoralized by its continual setbacks, and this led to court plots. This unease eventually led to disorder in the ranks and the fighting was brought to a close by the Convention of Bergara (1839), which did not openly threaten the Basque *fueros*. While General Cabrera resisted for another ten months, Don Carlos fled to France.

The queen mother, Maria Cristina, entrusted the government to General Espartero, who had defeated the Carlists, and, eventually, renounced the regency in his favor. Later, Espartero, under pressure from the liberals, had to abandon power and take refuge in England (1843) when Isabel II came to the throne.

Three years later, another civil war broke out, starting in Barcelona as a result of demonstations in support of a new Carlist pretender, Carlos Luis, known as Carlos VI, Count of Montemolin and youngest son of his predecesor, who had abdicated in his favor. Cabrera returned in 1847 to command the troops, but was forced to go back across the border the following year.

One of the Count of Montemolin's nephews, the son of his brother Juan and Maria Beatriz of Modena, relit the torch in 1868 under the name of Carlos VII. He started his struggle based in London, and later moved to Paris.

Four years later, during the reign of Amadeo I, who had succeeded Isabel II in 1871, matters became serious. The Convention of Amorebieta, which favored the charters, did not stop war from breaking out in 1873. Initially things went well for the Carlists when the First Republic, which was federalist in spirit, replaced Amadeo of Savoy. The Basque provinces were under their control, as was southern Araba (Arabako Errioxa/La Rioja Alavesa). Don Carlos was annointed king at Loiola [Loyola]. Courts were set up, as were military and scientific academies and a postal service, and the old University of Oñati [Oñate] was reopened.

However, after another siege of Bilbao, which became a setback for the Carlists, a new king of Spain was proclaimed in 1874: Alfonso XII. After a year, his generals, who had carried out successful campaigns in Catalonia, forced Don Carlos to recross the border at Arnegi [Arnéguy] (February 1876).[24]

Some months later, the *fueros* were suspended. The law introduced military recruitment, a territorial tax, payment of rights on mines and salt, the use of *papier timbré*, and replaced *foral* organizations with provincial councils like those throughout Spain.

Following this setback, the Bizkaian Sabino Arana Goiri, who had been a Carlist, founded the Basque Nationalist Party under the motto *Jaungoikoa eta Lege Zaharrak* (God and the Old Laws: in other words, the *fueros*). Meanwhile, the liberal government was facing considerable demands from the workers. After the death of Arana Goiri, in the early twentieth century, the movement became more radical as it lost its religious emphasis (for example, the Aberri eta Askatasuna (Homeland and Freedom) group, founded in 1910, and Acción Nacionalista Vasca/Eusko Abertzale Ekintza (Basque Patriotic Action)).

At the 1918 elections, seven nationalists, all of whom were calling for the reinstatement of the Basque *fueros*, were elected to the Spanish parliament (the *Cortes*). During Primo de Rivera's dictatorship, their movement was somewhat overshadowed, but not inactive: they organized and worked in favor of Basque cultural production (painting, music).

---

24. This defeat did not lead to the disappearance of Carlism, which had always had supporters for its pretenders from the traditionalist line, and which remains active.

In 1930, at the Pact of Donostia-San Sebastián, the autonomists restated their aims. The Euzkadi Buru Batzarra (The Supreme Council of the Basque Country), created in 1906 by the Basque Nationalist Communion (later Party), named the Bizkaian Jose Antonio Agirre its spokesman in the 1931 Spanish parliament, which had a Socialist and Republican majority. It had been summoned after the abdication of Alfonso XIII, the previous king's son, in favor of the Republic.

Agirre presented a proposal, which had been approved by the "grand assembly of town councils" held in Lizarra, for drawing up statutes of autonomy for the Basque provinces. The hardliners, though, wanted to use violence. However, the nationalist party gave its support to President Alcalá Zamora, which led to the Navarrese branch of the party splitting off.

In 1932 the first *Aberri Eguna* (Homeland Day) was celebrated, proclaiming the unity of the four provinces. The social unrest that shook northern Spain in October 1934 led to the party losing some seats in parliament to Frente Popular (Popular Front). However, these two movements were still allies and voted together in support of Manuel Azaña.

In July 1936, Spanish troops in Morocco rebelled and started the Civil War. The Basque Nationalist Party chose to support the Republic, while in Navarre the Carlist *Requetés* (milicia solidiers) and the provincial governor, General Mola, a friend of Franco's, gave all their support to the rebels. Thus, the northern front of the war separated the latter province from the pro-Republic *Vascongada* provinces. Gipuzkoa was conquered with the objective of preventing the Basque forces access to the French border.

A Basque government was formed in October 1936 under Agirre's leadership. However, the other side was stronger and one should not forget that Gernika, the "symbol of the *fueros*,"[25]

---

25. Gernika is a small historic city, the original heart of Bizkaia, where monarchs used to swear loyalty to the *fueros* under an oak tree (the sacred tree par excellence in Western Europe), which is carefully protected by a monument, and which had been grafted in 1860. This oak tree is on the Bizkaian coat of arms over a Latin cross that represents faith.

which was under Basque nationalist control, was destroyed by bombs dropped by German planes in April 1937. The Basque armies resisted surrendering for a long time and it was from Santander, where they had withdrawn to, that Agirre took a plane[26] to Biarritz on his way to exile.

The Northern Provinces: The French Revoluation and its Consequences; The Consulate and the Empire

The northern Basque provinces sent members to the 1789 Estates-General chosen by bailiwick (Zuberoa), by traditional assembly (the Estates of Navarre), and by specific processes (Lapurdi) through which the Basques obtained a separate bailiwick to that of Lannes (i.e., Les Landes), which they were part of. There, the *Biltzarra* chose the two Garat brothers, who were the only ones to leave their mark on the revolutionary annals.

The collective euphoria of the August Decrees carried the Basque members (except for the member for Lower Navarre, who did not sit) to vote, along with the others, for the abolition of priviledges. In other words, they ended up voting against all the particular freedoms and rights that their provinces had traditionally held.

After a moment of stupor and some reactions, especially from Lapurdi, the Basque provinces, including Lower Navarre, accepted joining the whole of France, and even losing their geographical personality by becoming part of Basses-Pyrénées. In practice, the ancient boundaries were not erased by this: many of the new territorial units reflected ancient demarcations.

One winner was the Basque language, which was used for writing all the texts that were going to be read by the people: until then, the Béarnais dialect had always been used as the official language by local administration.

Revolutionary as it was, the new regime could not resist committing excesses. Some of these did not involve the people actually suffering, and were rather picturesque, such as the practice of

---

26. The airplane's name was *Euzkadi*.

debaptizing places in order to give them names more in line with the
fashion of the times: Nive-Franche, Union, Thermopyles, Marat-
sur-Nive, and Chauvin-Dragon (the name of a local hero) replaced
Donibane Garazi, Itsasu [Itxassou], Baigorri, Uztaritze, and Donibane Lohizune respectively. Voting for a civil, lay constitution had
a deeper influence on the land: there were many unyielding priests
and the authorities were severe with them. While religion itself was
condemned, religious buildings and objects were also damaged: for
example, the tombs in Baiona cathedral.

One last characteristic allows us to see the ferocity of certain
revolutionary excesses. In 1794, and causing undescribable suffering, all the inhabitants of six villages in Lapurdi near the border
were deported to Les Landes and Gers in order to punish fifty
young people from Itsasu for deserting from military service. The
thing was that war with Spain had started again in 1792 because
menacing troop movements had been seen near the border. After
the French had spent more than a year in purely defensive positions
(tactics justified by an obvious numerical disadvantage), but which
did not stop the Basque "light infantry" from winning themselves
a reputation, the Army of the Western Pyrenees recruited volun-
teers en masse, attacked in 1794, occupied Baztan and Gipuzkoa,
where separatist fever reawoke, and, the following year, Bizkaia
and Araba. The Peace of Basel saved Navarre from the invasion it
had been threatened with.

Thereafter, the French Basque Country was the stage for some
dramatic events in the history of the two neighboring countries
(the confrontation between Napoleon and Carlos IV of Spain in
Baiona; imperial troops retreating under pressure from Welling-
ton), but it played no independent role in them. Which does not
mean that the situation was to remain as it was.

Appraisal and Outlook

Since those times, the Basques have, in fact, been less resigned to
giving up their demands than ever, to obtaining official recognition
for the "Basque phenomenon" that would allow them to safeguard
their personality and remain faithful to their destiny.

To the south of the Pyrenees, there are economic resources, several industries in Bizkaia that are essential for the Peninsula. Natural resources in other provinces, in contrast, are largely under exploited, which has led to emigration. Neither the Basque language nor Basque culture has any type of official recognition nor are they protected by public authorites.

Separatist and autonomist movements, which are more or less clandestine, such as ETA (Euskadi ta Askatasuna: the Basque Country and Freedom) often use violence, have their own martyrs and will always have a certain popular support, minority but efficient. Experiences during the last world war, the *maquis* (anti-Franco guerillas) and liberation have made militants familiar with subversive war techniques. The border is easier to cross than ever, despite official measures that, on the other hand, seem contrary to the political systems on both sides of the Pyrenees.

The Basques can make out the solution for their old problems in today's Europe. Centralizing policies, which have done them so much harm, could one day give way to a new ethical situation influenced by the existence of vast economic areas. A "Europe of the Peoples" is federalist in spirit, and while national boundaries may not be immediately erased, they will tend, at least temporarily, to open up just as they have to an extent in the context of the Common Market and Comecon. This will allow a cultural regrouping that, without endangering the power of states that have never previously been linked, will save the enriching differences that have shaped our civilization.

The Basque ethnic group, which, with its old language, has had an exceptional destiny over thousands of years and has kept itself from disappearing, will find its sustenance there. May its history be written at last (and it is high time!) in terms of resistence, future, and hope.

Part 3

Language and Literature

The Language

Outline of the Linguistic System

General Considerations

If the Basque language (Euskara or, in French Basque, Eskuara) can define the ethnic group that speaks it, this is because, as far as we know, it is a completely isolated language in Europe and, indeed, in the whole world. Any analysis of the language reveals structures that are out of the ordinary in the world of "Western" linguistics; structures whose essential characteristics we will try to explain in this section. After a brief description, a short bilingual passage will enable the reader to get a better idea of the language.

Like all natural languages, it varies from one region to another and the dialects, in general, correspond to the old provinces. From west to east, the dialects are: Bizkaian, whose particularities have led some linguists to place it in its own separate group; Gipuzkoan, which, until now, has been the main literary dialect in Spain; Lapurdian, which, along with Lower Navarrese, is favored by writers in France; Zuberoan, an old dialect that is also influenced by Gascon (spoken accent; letter *ü*); Upper Navarrese, in Spain, is dying out and has never had a literary tradition.

Nowadays Standard or Unified Basque (Euskara Batua) is being drawn from these heterogeneous dialects, and is very close to Lapurdian, which we take as our model in this section.

Sounds

This is the least original aspect of the language. There are five vowels, as in Castilian: *a, e, I, o,* and *u* ('*ou*' in French): *hala,* 'like that'; *hela* 'to pull', verb root; *hila,* 'dead,' adjective; *hola,* 'just like this'; *hula,* 'like this'.

There are descending dipthongs:

Dipthongs endings in *u*: *au* (*lau,* 'four'); *eu* (*beude,* 'let them stay where they are').

Dipthongs endings in *i*: *ai* (*bai,* 'yes'); *ei* (*sei,* 'six'); *oi* (*hogoi,* 'twenty'); *ui* (*muin,* 'marrow').

There are no nasal vowels.

There are voiceless consonants: *p* (*eper,* 'partridge'); *t* (*ate,* 'door'); *k* (*aker,* 'billy goat'); voiced consonants: *b* (*abar,* 'little branch'); *d* (*adar,* 'horn'); *g* (*egur,* 'firewood');

Nasal consonants: *m* (*ama,* 'mother'); *n* (*ene,* 'my');

Three series of sibilants:

s, a special sound, similar to the *s* in Spanish but more hissing (*oso,* 'entire');

z, like *s* in French (*aza,* 'cabbage');

x, similar to *ch* in French (*xori,* 'bird');

these are often affected by the preceding letters, either fricative or affricate consonants (*etsai,* 'enemy'; *atzo,* 'yesterday'; *etxe* 'house');

The lateral consonant *l* (*ala,* 'or'); the resonant *r,* which can be single or double (*ere,* 'also'; *erre* 'burned');

The aspirated consonant *h,* which is unknown in Spain (*han,* 'there'; *aho,* 'mouth');

And, finally, specific palatal or 'moistened' consonants, which vary in sound: *tt* (similar to *ch,* as in "chew"); *j* (voiced: *jo,* 'to hit'); and, in certain dialects, the 'moistened' *l,* sometimes written *ll* (*pollit,* 'pretty'); and the 'moistened' *n,* sometimes written as *ñ* (*muña,* a variant of *muina,* 'marrow').

There is no noticeable accent in each word.

Noun and Pronoun Inflection

Patterns of Inflection

Like Finnish, Hungarian, and Turkish, in Basque, nouns, pronouns, and adjectives are "declined" by adding suffixes to an unchanging root (there is a single exception: each of the three demonstrative pronouns is formed using three different roots). Some suffixes can be added to other suffixes ("subdeclension": see below). Only the last part of the noun phrase is "declined," the rest remaining in their basic forms (see morpho-syntax).

There is no grammatical gender. On the other hand, there are two types of inflection: the *indeterminate*, in which the noun is not specified, and the *determinate*, which includes a singular and a plural and generally has an item after it (often called the article). However, it is often impossible to distinguish between case and determinate suffixes.

Cases and Their Marks

The twelve cases have suffixes that are unchanging whatever the root and type (noun, pronoun, or adjective) of the word declined:

1. Nominative. Subjects of intransitive verbs, direct objects of transitive verbs, and their attributes: no suffix and –ak in plural.
2. Ergative. Subjects of transitive verbs: suffix –k.
3. Instrumental. Means by which things are done or made: suffix –z.
4. Dative. Those who receive the action: suffix –i.
5. Genitive possessive. Ownership: suffix –en.
6. Comitative. Accompaniment: suffix –ekin.
7. Prolative. Destination: suffix –tzat ('instead of') and –entzat ('for').
8. Genitive locative. Position in time or space: suffix –ko.
9. Inessive. Place where something is: suffix –n.
10. Lative. Place where something is going: suffix –rat.
11. Elative. Place from which something is coming: suffix –tik.
12. Partitive. Suffix *–ik*.

Forming Paradigms

In indeterminate inflections, suffixes are added directly to the root (personal and place names), and, in the locative, preceded by the infix –*ta*-.

In the singular, *a* (the "article") is placed between the root and the suffix except for in cases 8, 10, and 11.

In the plural, the determiner is *e* (except for in case 1, which takes the general suffix –*ak*) and the infix –*ta*- is placed between it and the suffixes in cases 8–11, as in the indeterminate (after –*ta*-, the elative suffix –*tik* is replaced with –*rik*).

In the interests of phonoaesthetics, hiatuses before suffixes are solved by including an –*r*-, and double consonants are solved by including an –*e*-. When there are two *a*'s together, they merge, but roots finishing in –*a* lose that *a* to the plural *e*. The inessive singular always finishes in –*an*, except when this becomes –*ean* after a consonant.

Our examples are Baigorri and *xori*, 'bird':

		Indeterminate	Singular	Plural
1.	Baigorri	xori	xori-a	xori-ak
2.	Baigorri-k	xori-k	xori-a-k	xori-e-k
3.	Baigorri-z	xori-z	xori-a-z	xori-e-(ta)-z
4.	Baigorri-r-i	xori-r-i	xori-a-r-i	xori-e-r-(i)/-ei
5.	Baigorri-r-en	xori-r-en	xori-a-r-en	xori-en (no 'r'!)
6.	Baigorri-r-ekin	xori-r-ekin	xori-a-r-ekin	xori-ekin (ditto)
7.	Baigorri-(r-en)tzat	xori-(r-en)tzat	xori-a-r-en-tzat	xori-en-tzat (ditto)
8.	Baigorri-ko	xori-ta-ko	xori-ko	xori-e-ta-ko
9.	Baigorri-n	xori-ta-n	xori-an	xori-e-ta-n
10.	Baigorri-rat	xori-ta-rat	xori-rat	xori-e-ta-rat
11.	Baigorri-tik	xori-ta-rik	xori-tik	xori-e-ta-rik
12.	Baigorri-r-ik	xori-r-ik	(none)	(none)

This is also so for the three nominatives and ergatives:
seme, 'son': *sem-e-k, seme-a, seme-a-k, seme-ak, seme-e-k*
bero, 'hot': *bero-k, bero-a, bero-a-k, bero-ak, bero-ek*
buru, 'head': *buru-k, buru-a, buru-a-k, buru-ak, buru-e-k*
basa, 'savage': *basa-k, basa, basa-k (-a + a > a), basa-k, bas-e-k*
on, 'good': *on-e-k, on-a, on-a-k, on-ak, on-e-k*
zahar, 'old': *zaharr-e-k, zaharr-a, zaharr-a-k, zaharr-ak, zaharr-e-k,*
etc.

Pronominal Inflections and Complementary Indications

The pronominal adjectives are clearly formed in the same way. There are three demonstrative pronouns, each one forming its inflections based on three roots. The forms for nearest things and beings is the nominative singular *hau*, the other singular cases being based on *hun-*, the plural on *haui-* (nominative *hauk*). The forms for things and beings at a medium distance are *hori*, *horr-*, and *hoi-*. The forms for far-off things and beings are *hura*, *har-*, and *he(i)-*, which is also the non-reflexive third person anaphoric pronoun.

True personal pronouns refer to people in a dialogue: first person singluar *ni* (genitive possessive *nere/ene*); second person singular *hi*; first person plural *gu*; polite form second person plural (but with singular meaning) *zu*; second person plural (and with plural meaning) *zuek*. Their genitive forms[1] are the possessive pronouns, to which the reflexive forms *bere* (singular) and *beren* (plural) are added.

The interrogative pronouns are derived from two main themes: *ze-*, 'what' and *no-*, 'who'. This gives us *zer*, 'what'; *zein/zoin*, 'which'; *nor*, 'who'; *non*, 'where'; *noiz*, 'when'; *nola*, 'how,' and so forth.

The variety of the indefinite pronouns derives from their lexical sources: compounds of *–bait* (*zerbait*, 'something'; *norbait*, 'someone,' and so on) and compounds of *edo-/-nahi* (*edozer/zernahi*, 'whatever'); negative forms are compounds of *ne-* (*nehor*, 'nobody'; *nehon*, 'nowhere').

The numbers are based on a vigesimal system.

Cardinal numbers: *bat* (1), *bi(ga)* (2), *hiru(r)* (3), *lau(r)* (4), *bortz/bost* (5), *sei* (6), *zazpi* (7), *zortzi* (8), *bederatzi* (9), *hamar* (10), *hameka* (11), *hamabi* (12), *hamahiru* (13), and so on; *hogoi* (20), *hogoi-ta-hamar* (30), *berrogoi* (40); *hiruretan-hogoi* (60); *hiruetan-hogoi-ta-hamar* (70), and so on; *ehun* (100), *mila* (1000).

Ordinal numbers: after *lehen* (first), these are formed using the suffix *–garren*: *bigarren*, *hirugarren*, and so on.

Pronouns are often formed using the indeterminate (for example, *huntarik*, *gutarik*, *zertarik*).

---

1. Archaic forms without *–n*: *hire, gure, zure* (but real plural *zuen*).

Finally, a word about degrees of comparison. Comparatives are formed with the suffix *–ago* (*zahar*, 'old' > *zaharrago*, 'older'; however, *on*, 'good' > *hobe*, 'better'). Superlatives are formed with the suffix *–en* (*zaharren-a*, 'the oldest'; *hoberen-a*, 'the best'). The excessive is formed using the suffix *–egi* (*zaharr-egi*, 'too old').

Verb Inflections

The Foundations of the System

Its most original feature is the pluripersonality of the personal verb forms: in other words, rather than only varying depending on the subject, as in other European languages, they also include markers that refer to other participants in the action. The direct object is mentioned whenever a transitive verb is used as, in some cases, is the beneficiary of the action with both transitive and intransitive verbs. For example, *jiten zira*, 'you come' (from *jin*, 'to come'), but *jiten zatzaizkit*, 'you come to me'; *emaiten duzu*, 'you give it' ('you give' by itself is impossible to say), but *emaiten dautazu*, 'you give it to me' (from *eman*, 'to give').

With regard to verb forms and tenses, Basque uses morphological structures (for simple and synthetic forms) that are based on two opposites: on the one hand, the "(simple) present" as opposed to the "non-present" that, in turn, divides into "(simple) past" and "potential" and, on the other hand, the "realis" as opposed to the "potential."

For example, the third person singular of the verb *egon*, 'to remain':

		Real	Potential
	Present	*dago* there is	*dagoke* there could be
Non-present	Past	*zegon* there was	*zegoken* there could have been
	Possible	*(ba)lago* if there were	*lagoke* there would be

The future and all other verb modalities and tenses are periphrastic (see below).

Personal Markers

These are formed using prefixes when, on the one hand, for subject in the non-present and the object is third person singular or plural; on the other hand, objects of transitive verbs except for in the cases just mentioned. They are formed using suffixes for the beneficiaries of intransitive verbs and agents of transitive verbs (with the previously mentioned exceptions), while beneficiaries, when there are such, come immediately before the latter.

For example, *n*ago, '*I* remain'; *nau*zu, 'you have *me*' ('me' as the direct object), but *zin*uen, '*you* had it'; zai*t*, 'it is for/to *me*'; *nau*zu, 'you have *me*'; dau*t*zazu, 'you have it (for *me*).

It is important to note that the same person cannot participate more than once, so there are no reflexive verb forms (of course, this question does not arise for the third person singular and plural when different people are being referred to!)

Grammatical Person Forms

		Prefixes		Suffixes
1st sing	present	*n-*		*t*
	others	*nind-*		
2nd sing	present	*h-*		{ *k* (masc)
	others	*hind-*		{ *n* (fem)
3rd sing	present	*d-*		{ ø (subject)
	past	*z-*		{ *(k)o* (beneficiary)
	conditional	*l-*		
1st plur	present	*g-*	*z-* ***	*gu*
	others	{ *gin-*	*z-*	
		{ *gind-*	*z-*	
2nd plur (polite form)	present	*z-*	*zte-*	*zu*
	others	{ *zin-*	*zte-*	
		{ *zind-*	*zte-*	
2nd plur (plural)	present	*z-*	*zte-*	*zue*
	others	{ *zin-*	*zte-*	
		{ *zind-*	*zte-*	
3rd plur	present	*d-*	*z-*	{ *te* (subject)
	past	*z-*	*z-*	{ *(k)ote, e* (beneficiary)
	conditional	*l-*	*z-*	

*** -*z*-, in this case, is a marker which makes the prefixes plural. For example, *doa*, he/she goes, becomes *doatzi*, 'they go'; *dakit*, 'I know,' *dazkit, dakizkit, dakitzat*, 'I know them'; *duzu*, 'you have it,' *dituzu*, 'you have them,' etc.

To this already complex scheme we must add the possibility of the speaker including a marker for his/her interlocutor in the verb if he/she is not already involved in the process: the allocutive. For example, *ikusten dut* (from *ikusi*, 'to see'), 'I see it' becomes *ikusten di(k)at* in the masculine intimate form (in which the interlocutor is male) and *ikusten dinat* in the feminine form (in which the interlocutor is female), and so on. (However, *ikusten haut*, 'I see you' and *ikusten nauk*, 'you see me,' obviously do not undergo this morphological modification.)

Periphrastic Conjugation: The Four Auxiliary Verbs

Only the auxiliary verbs and a few frequently used verbs follow the six patterns shown above. All other verbs combine an invariable nominal or adjectival form. Participles can be marked to express a perfect state with the conjugated auxiliary verbs, so:

a verb with	*dago*	is similar to	*igaiten da*, 'he/she goes up' (*da*, 'he/she is')
"	*zegon*	"	*igaiten zen*, 'he/she was going up' (*zen*, 'he/she was')
"	*(ba)lago*	"	*igaiten balitz*, 'if he/she went up' (*balitz*, 'if he/she was')

in which *igaiten* is an old inessive form of the the verb *igaite*, 'to go up.'

The past participle *igan* is used to construct *igan da*, 'he/she has gone up' (if the determined past participle is used, *igana da*, it means 'he/she has just gone up, he/she is up there'); *igan zen*, 'he/she was going up, went up.' The future is formed using the genitive of the past participle in conjunction with the auxiliary in the realis present form, *iganen* (genitive possessive) *da*, 'he/she will go up'; *ibiliko* (genitive locative) *da*, 'he/she will walk' (from *ibili*, 'to walk'). In the same way, *iganen zen*, 'he/she was going to walk,' is the future-in-the-past, and so forth.

With regard to the auxiliary verbs, as well as the forms of *izan*, 'to be' (*da, zen, balitz*) and *ukan*, 'to have' (*dut, haut, zinuen, nauk*), which we have already seen, we must complete the table with two other defective Basque auxiliary verbs that, depending on their use, state wishes, objectives, orders, or possibilities. Their stems are *di-* (without any participle) for intransitive verbs and *za-* for transitive verbs and in French Basque they are used with the "minimal form" of the conjugated verb, the simple verb root: *geldi hadi*, 'stay still!' (from *gelditu*, 'to stay still'); *garbi zazu*, 'clean it!' (from *garbitu*, 'to clean'[2]); *geldi litake*, 'they would clean it' (tomorrow); *garbi lezake*, 'they would clean it' (ibid); *etzezaken garbi*, 'they were unable to clean it' (past potential), and so on.

Now, as an example, see some verb forms:

2. *Garbi* is an adjective meaning 'clean, pure'; *garbitu* is derived from it.

Izan (to be), Simple Present

Uni-personal

Subject	
1	naiz
2	haiz
3	da
4	gare
5	zare
5'	zarezte
6	dire

Multi-personal

Beneficiary →

Subject	1	2 (masc)	2 (fem)	3	4	5	5'	6
1	ø	nitzaik	nitzain	nitzaio	ø	nitzaiztu	nitzaiztue	nitzaiote
2	hitzait	ø	ø	hitzaio	hitzaiku	ø	ø	hitzaiote
3	zait	zaik	zain	zaio	zaiku	zaitzu	zaitzue	zaiote
4	ø	gitzaizkik	gitzaizkin	gitzaizkio	ø	gitzaizkitzu	gitzaizkitzue	gitzaizkiote
5	zitzaizkit	ø	ø	zitzaizkio	zitzaizkigu	ø	ø	zitzaizkiote
5'	zitzaizkidate	ø	ø	zitzaizkiote	zitzaizkigute	ø	ø	zitzaizkiote
6	zaizkit	zaizkik	zaizkin	zaizkio	ziazkigu	zaizkitzu	zaizkitzue	zaizkiote

Ukan (to have), Simple Present

Subject →

Object	1	2 (masc)	2 (fem)	3	4	5	5'	6
1	ø	nauk	naun	nau	ø	nauzu	nauzue	naute
2	haut	ø	ø	hau	haugu	ø	ø	haute
3	dut	duk	dun	du	dugu	duzu	duzue	dute
4	ø	gaituk	gaitun	gaitu	ø	gaituzu	gaituzue	gaituzte
5	zaitut	ø	ø	zaitu	zaitugu	ø	ø	zaituzte
5'	zaituztet	ø	ø	zaituzte	zaituztegu	ø	ø	zaituzte (1)
6	ditut	dituk	ditun	ditu	ditugu	ditutzu	ditutzue	dituzte

(1) This form should be 'zaituztete,' but such cacophonous forms give way to multipurpose forms such as 'zaituzte,' any ambiguity being cleared up by the context.

Because tripersonal intransitive forms are only possible with a 3rd person singular or plural direct object, the triple variation is, in fact, reduced to two systems with double entries:

Subject	Beneficiary →							
	1	2 (masc)	2 (fem)	3	4	5	5'	6
1	ø	dau(k)at	daunat	diot	ø	dautzut	dautzuet	diotet
2 (masc)	dautak	ø	ø	diok	daukuk	ø	ø	diotek
2 (fem)	dautan	ø	ø	dion	daukun	ø	ø	dioten
3	daut	dauk	daun	dio	dauku	dautzu	dautzue	diote
4	ø	dau(k)agu	daunagu	diogu	ø	dautzugu	dautzuegu	diotegu
5	dautazu	ø	ø	diozu	daukuzu	ø	ø	diotezu
5'	dautazue	ø	ø	diozue	daukuzue	ø	ø	diotezue
6	dautate	dau(k)ate	daunate	diote	daukute	dautzute	dautzeute	diote

As in the case mentioned above, the form 'diote' is multipurpose. If the object is third person plural, an infix is used: 'dautak' becomes 'dauzkidak' (with 'ki' added for the sake of euphony) and 'diot' becomes 'diozkit/diozkat/diotzat,' etc.

Morphosyntaxis

We have already seen, in general terms, the main features of Basque morphology, but there is still much to say. While the organization and positioning of parts of the sentence are the key to simple sentences, it is in complex sentences that you really see the important of affixes in Basque, taking on, as they do, functions carried out by subordinate clauses in other languages.

Noun Phrases

There are two main principles:

All objects, except for attributive adjectives, go before the verb. Only the second member of a series of juxtaposed or coordinated terms with the same grammatical function is determined and declined (for example, *harotzaren etxea*, 'the blacksmith's house' (*harotz*, 'blacksmith'), but *etxe xuria*, 'the white house'; *etxe handi eta eder bat*, 'a big and beautiful house'; *etxe handi eta ederraren izena*, 'the name of the big and beautiful house.'

As case suffixes do not explain precisely all nuances in all cases, there are numerous postpositions, in other words, declined nouns that are preceded by noun determinators: *oihanari buruz*, 'toward the wood' (*oihan*), in which *buruz* in the instrumental single of *buru*, 'head,' determined by a dative noun; *etxearen aintzinean*, 'in front of the house,' in which *ainzin*, 'front part' in inessive singular, is determined by a genitive possessive noun. One of the terms may be left undeclined: *zuri* (dative) *esker* (nominative), 'thanks to you'; *etze-aintzinean* (see above), with *etxe-aintzin* being treated as a compound noun.

Both types of genitive can be used to create derived forms that, in turn, can be declined with case suffixes. While *harotzaren etxea* is 'the blacksmith's house,' *harotzarena* is 'the blacksmith's one,' and one can also say *harotzarenaren izena*, 'the name of the blacksmith's one,' and so on. Likewise, *etxeko atea* is 'the house's door' and *etxekoa* is 'the house's one,' and so forth. However, comparing the latter to the former example, the suffix *–ko* can be added to many other suffixes, thus forming the derived noun par excellence: after an instrumental (*urre*, 'gold,' *urrez*, 'with gold,' *urrezko* *erraztuna*, 'the golden ring'; *euskarazko liburua*, 'the book written in Basque'), a lative (*etxetikako bidea*, 'the path that comes from the house'), a comitative (*harotzarkilako gizona*, 'the man who is with the blacksmith'),[3] and so on.

Verb Phrases

Positioned at the end of the phrase because it is determined by all the other elements, the verbal predicate neccessarily takes into account the main participants in each phrase.

It is here that we see another highly orginal feature of the Basque language: the ergative. Intransitive verbs are only related to the subject and, occasionally, to the beneficiary; transitive verbs, on the other hand, have to be related to the subject (or agent) and the direct object, and may also have a beneficiary. But while the subject of an intransitive verb is given no specific case mark (it is nominative, an unmarked case), with transitive verbs the active participant (the subject or agent) is given a positive mark, the ergative, while the object is nominative and, as such, unmarked.

This structure is echoed in the order of elements used to make up synthetic verbs: being nominative, the subject of transitive verbs and the object of intransitive verbs are both prefixes: *nago*, 'I remain'; *nakar*, 'he/she takes *me*' (*ekarri*, 'take'). Naturally, the beneficiary is always dative.

Subordinate Phrases

With the same role as subordinate phrases in other languages, there are affixes attached to conjugated verbs that link subordinate verbs to the main clause verb. One should remember that the determining clause usually precedes the clause that it determines.

The suffix *–n* plays a triple role:
1. Making relative clauses. *Etxea erosi dut*, 'I have bought the house' > *erosi dudan etxea*, 'the house I have bought' and,

---

3. We cannot resist quoting a word (and what a word!) that P. Lafitte records a child saying when his mother asked him who he had been playing with: *Ponetarekila-koarekin*, 'With he who has the beret (*ponet*).' As simple as that.

of course, *erosi dudana*, 'the one I have bought,' and so on. See below.

2. Linking main clauses to subordinate clauses when there is a verb expressing will or an indirect question: *nahi dut egin dezaten* (auxiliary *za-*), 'I want them to do it,' *zer egiten dute?*, 'what are they doing?' > *galdegiten diotet zer egiten duten*, 'I ask what they are doing.'

3. In the inessive singular, transforming a sentence into a time subordinate clause: *hasten da*, 'it begins' > *hasten denean*, 'when it begins.'

The suffix *–la* plays a double role:

1. Simply connecting the main clause to the subordinate: *badakizu erosi dudala*, 'you know that I have bought it.'

2. With various different suffixes, forming other types of subordinates. Time clauses: *hasten delarik*, 'when it begins.' Clauses expressing cause ending in *–lakotz*: *erosi dudala-kotz*, 'because I have bought it.'

The prefix *(balin)ba-* expresses conditions, as we have already seen: *xuria ba(linba)da, erosiko dut*, 'if it is white, I will buy it'; *xuria ba(linba)litz, ederragoa litake*, 'if it were white, it would be more beautiful; *eros baneza*, 'if I bought it (tomorrow).'

The prefix *bait-* has various related uses that can be both relative and express cause and time: *etxe hori erosi dut, xuria baitzen*, 'I have bought that house as/because it was white.'

Content Analysis

We are going to illustrate our description using a translation of the Parable of the Prodigal Son into Lapurdian Basque.[4] After the English [French in the original—ed.] text and its Basque translation you will be able to see the two texts juxtapositioned line-by-line, and this will make it possible to see the details of work.

The following conventions have been used:

---

4. Cf. Pierre Bec's *La langue occitane*, in the *Qué sais-je?* collection, no. 1059.

Noun and pronoun declensions are marked by a combination of letters as previously explained: NOM – Nominative; ERG – Ergative; INS – Instrumental; DAT – Dative; GENP – Genitive Possessive; COM – Comitative; PROL – Prolative; GLOC – Genitive Locative; INE – Inessive; LAT – Lative; ELA – Elative; PTV – Partitive (the text has neither comitatives nor prolatives); I – indeterminate; S – singular; P – plural.

As far as verb conjugation is concerned, personal forms of auxiliary verbs are marked as follows: SPr – Simple Present; SPa – Simple Past; Part – Participle; H – Hypothetical; R – Realis; Pot – Potential; Root – Root; and Imp – Imperative. Grammatical persons are numbered from 1 to 6 with 5t being the "true plural" and 5p being the "polite plural"; "m" and "f" represent, respectively, the male and female "you" form; and order of the participants is: for intransitive verbs, subject ___ (beneficiary); for transitive verbs, agent ___ object ___ (beneficiary).

English Text

A man had no more than two sons.

The youngest said to his father: "It is time for me to control my own fate and have some money. It is time for me to leave here to see places; divide your riches and give me what is mine!"

"My son," his father said to him, "as you like! You are a bad lad and you will be punished."

And then he opened a drawer, divided his riches and made two lots.

A few days later, the bad lad left the village, puffed up, and without saying goodbye to anyone.

He crossed many fields, woods, and rivers.

Some months later, he had to sell his clothes to an old woman and become a servant. They sent him out to the fields to look after donkeys and oxen. Then he was truly sorry: no bed to sleep in at night, and no fire to warm him when it was cold. Sometimes he was so hungry that he was glad to eat the cabbage leaves and rotten fruit that pigs eat. But nobody gave him anything.

One afternoon, with an empty belly, he sat on a tree trunk and looked through the window at the birds flying in the air. And later, when he saw the moon and the stars come out in the sky, he cried as he said to himself:

"There, my father's house is full of servants who can have as much bread and wine as they want; and, all the while, I am dying of hunger here. Hence, I will get up and go to my father and say to him:

"When I went away from you I sinned. I made a mistake, and you must punish me for that, I know that well. Call me your son no longer. Treat me like your lowliest servant. I was guilty, but far from you I found no pleasure!'"

Basque Text

Gizon batek bi seme baizik etzituen.

Gazteenak bere aitari erran zion: "Ordu dut ene buruaren jabe izaitea eta zerbait diru izaitea. Joan behar nuke hemendik bazterren ikusterat; zure ontasuna parti zazu eta heldu zaitzana eman!"

"Ene semea," erran zion aitak, "nahi dukan bezala! Mutiko tzar bat haiz eta gaztigatua izanen haiz."

Eta gero tireta bat ideki zuen, bere ontasuna partitu eta bi parti egin.

Handik zenbait egunen buruan, mutiko tzarra herritik joan zen, espantuka eta nehori adiorik egin gabe.

Frango larre, oihan eta ur pasatu zituen.

Zenbait hilabeteren buruan, bere arropak emazteki xahar bati saldu behar izatu zituen, eta mutil sartu zen. Landetarat igorri zuten asto eta idi zain. Orduan ederrak pekatu zituen: gauaz oherik ez lo egiteko, eta ez surik ere hotza zagolarik berotzeko. Zonbait aldiz hain gose zen nun zerriek jaten dituzten aza osto eta fruitu ustelak gogotik janen baitzituen; baina nehork etzion deusik emaiten.

Arats batez, tripa hutsik, trunko batean gainean jarri zen, leihotik begira airetan ibiliki ziren xorieri. Eta gero, ilhargia eta izarrak zeruan agertzen ikusi zituen, eta nigarrez bere baitan egin zuen:

"Han, ene aitaren etxea nahi bezenbat ogi eta arno, arroltze eta gasna duten mutilez betea da; denbora hortan, ni goseak hila nago hemen. Are, xutituko naiz, ene aitaren ganat joanen naiz eta erranen diot:

'Zutaz urrundu nahi bainuen bekatu egin nuen. Hobendu nuen, eta hortaz gaztigatu behar nauzu, badakit ontsa; ez nezazu gehiago zure semea deit; zure azken mutila bezala trata nezazu; hobendun nintzen, bainan zutarik urrun ez nuen laketzen!'"

Juxtalinear Translation

Gizon⁵	batek	bi	seme	baizik		etzituen.
Man	a (ERG I)	two	son	no more than		*ez* (neg.) + *ukan* (Spa R36)

Gazteenak	bere	aitari	erran	zion:
Young (superl. ERG S)	his (refl.)	father (DAT S)	say (Part)	*ukan* (SPa R333)

"Ordu	dut	ene	buruaren	jabe	izaitea
Time	*ukan* (SPr R13)	me (GENP)	head (GENP S)	master	being (NOM S)

eta	zerbait	diru	izaitea.	Joan	behar	nuke
and	something	money	having (NOM S)	go (Part)	need	*ukan* (H Pot13)

hemendik	bazterren	ikusterat;	zure	ontasuna
here (ELA)	place (GENP P)	act of seeing (LAT S)	you (GENP)	riches (NOM S)

parti	zazu	eta	heldu⁶	zaitana	eman!"
divide (root)	*za-* (Imp 5p3)	come (Part)	*izan* (SPr R31) + rel. NOM S	give (Part-Root)	

"Ene semea,"	erran zion	aitak,	"nahi	dukan	bezala.
(NOM S)		(ERG S)	wish	*ukan* (SPr R2m3 + complement)	as

Mutiko	tzar	bat	haiz	eta	gaztigatua	izanen haiz."
lad	bad		*izan* (Spr R2)		punish (Part NOM S)	*izan* (Part GENP)

Eta	gero	tireta	bat	ideki	zuen,	bere ontasuna	partitu
	then	drawer		open (Part)	*ukan* (SPa R33)		(Part)

eta bi	parte	egin.	Handik	zenbait	egunen	buruan,
	lot	make	there (ELA)	some	day (GENP I)	end (INE S)

---

5. No inflection, indeterminate nominative.

6. *Heldu* has no participle value; *heldu da* means 'he/she comes.'

Handik   *zenbait*   *egunen*   *buruan,*   *mutiko*   *tzarra*
there (ELA)   some   day (GENP I)   end (INE S)   (NOM S)

herritik   *joan*   *zen,*   *espantuka*
village (ELA S)   *izan* (SPa R3)   arrogant + -*ka* adv.

eta   *nehori*   *adiorik*   *egin*   *gabe.*
       nobody (DAT)   goodbye (PTV)   without

Frango   *larre,*   *oihan*   *eta*   *ur*   *pasatu*   *zituen.*
many   land   wood   water   cross (Part)

Zenbait   *hilabeteren*   *buruan, bere*   *arropak*   *emazteki*   *xahar*
             month (GENP I)   clothes (NOM P)   woman   old (dimin.)

bati   *saldu*   *behar*   *izatu*   *zituen, eta*   *mutil*   *sartu*
(DAT I) sell (Part)   *izan* ('to have', perfect tense)   servant enter (Part)

zen. Landetarat   *igorri*   *zuten*   *asto*   *eta*   *idi*   *zain.*   *Orduan*
       field (LAT P) send (Part) *ukan* (SPa R63) donkey   ox   guard   (INE S)

ederrak   *pekatu*   *zituen:*[7]   *gauaz*   *oherik*   *ez*   *lo*
well (NOM P)   expiate (Part)   night (INS S)   bed (PTV)   sleep

egiteko,   *eta ez*   *surik*   *ere*   *hotza*
act of doing (GLOC S)   fire (PTV)   also   cold (NOM S)

zagolarik   *berotzeko.*   *Zonbait*   *aldiz*
remain (SPa R3) + temporal -*larik*   act of heating (GLOC S)   var. of *zenbait*   time (INS I)

hain   *gose*   *zen*   *nun*   *zerriek*   *jaten*
so   hunger/hungry   where, as conj. 'that'   pig (ERG P)   act of eating (INE I)

dituzten   *aza*   *osto eta fruitu*   *ustelak*   *gogotik*
ukan (SPr R66) + rel. cabbage   leaf   fruit   rotten (NOM P)   will(ingly) (ELA S)

janen   *baitzituen;*   *baina*   *nehork*   *etzion*   *deusik*
eat (Part GENP) pref. *bait-* + verb   but   nobody (ERG)   nothing (SPa)

emaiten.
act of giving (INE I)

---

7. A set phrase literally meaning "he pays the price."

The Basques   73

Arats   batez,   tripa   hutsik,   trunko batean   gainean[8]
afternoon (INS I) belly (NOM S) empty (PTV) trunk (GENP I) top (INE S)

jarri   zen,   leihotik   begira   airetan   ibiliki
sit (Part)   window (ELA S) look (Root) air (INE P) adv. der. from 'walk'

ziren.   xorieri.   Eta gero,   ilhargia   eta   izarrak
izan (SPa R6 + rel.) bird (DAT P)   moon (NOM S) and   star (NOM P)

zeruan   agertzen   ikusi   zituen, eta   nigarrez   bere
sky (INE S) act of appearing (INE I) see (Part)   cry (INS I)

baitan[9] *egin zuen:*
in

"*Han, ene   aitaren   etxea   nahi   bezenbat   ogi eta   arno,*
             (GENP S) house (NOM S)   as much (as) bread   wine

arroltze eta gasna   duten   mutilez   betea   da;   denbora
egg   cheese *ukan* (SPr R63) (INS I) full (NOM S) *izan* (SPr R3) time

hortan,   ni   goseak   hila   nago   hemen.
that (INE I) I (NOM S) (ERG S) kill/die (Part NOM S) remain (SPr R1) here

Are,   xutituko   naiz,   ene aitaren ganat[10] *joanen naiz eta*
hence get up (Part GLOC) *izan* (SPr R1) to the house (GENP)

erranen   diot:
(GENP)   *ukan* (SPr R133)

'*Zutaz   urrundu   nahi   bainuen   bekatu egin nuen.*
(INS I) go away (Part) pref. *bait-* + *ukan* (SPr R13)   sin

Hobendu   nuen, eta   hortaz   gaztigatu behar   nauzu,
make a mistake (Part)   (INS I)   *ukan* (SPR R5p1)

badakit   ontsa. Ez nezazu   gehiago   zure   semea
pref. *ba-* + know (SPr R13) well *za-* Imp 5p more   (NOM S)

deit;   zure azken mutila bezala   trata   nezazu; hobendun   nintzen,
call (Root)   last   treat (Root)   guilty *izan* (SPa R1)

---

8. The postposition *gainean* (with its corresponding *gainerat, gainetik, gaineko*, etc.) means simply "on," without any exceptions.

9. The postpositions *baitan, ganat,* and *ganik* replace the simple inessive, allative, and elative cases where people are concerned.

10. Ibid.

bainan	*zutarik*	*urrun*	*ez nuen*	*laketzen!'"*
	(ELA I)	far		pleasing (INE I)

Dialectology and History of the Language

Dialectology

Of the previously mentioned dialects, we have said that Bizkaian is unique in using the verb *egin*, 'to do,' instead of *za-* as the transitive auxiliary verb: it removes the prefix *z-* and replaces it with a zero prefix (no prefix) for the third and sixth persons in the past (*egoan*, 'he/she remained,' cf. *zegon*; *ebazan*, 'he/she had them,' cf. *zituen*), but using a pluralizing suffix instead of an infix (*dodaz*, 'I have them', cf. *ditut*. Also compare *dot/dut*, 'I have'). Bizkaian also uses *–e* instead of *–te* as the suffix for the third person plural (*dabe* cf. *dute*. Also cf. Zuberoan). In the bipersonal conjunction of *izan*, 'to be,' (making reference to the beneficiary), the root *za-* is replaced by *ya-* when the subject is third person singular or plural (*yako* cf. *zaio*, 'it is for him/her').

In Gipuzkoan the *h* is not aspirated. The nominative plural and ergative take the same form: *-ak*. The past subjunctive uses the past participle instead of the verb root. The genitive locative is used instead of the genitve posesive to form the future (*egingo* instead of *eginen*). There is a sort of passive past participe that is formed by adding the suffix *–ta-/-da-* to the participle and using the genitive locative (*ikusiktako gauzak*, 'the things seen'; *egindako lana*, 'the work done'). The lexeme *esan* is used instead of *erran*, 'to say.' In Gipuzkoan the plural form of the second person plural is formed using *–zute* rather than *–zue*. The vowel *e* is used instead of *u* in the present of *ukan*[11] except for the third person (*det, dezu*; however, *du, dute*). The root *–i-* is generally used in the tripersonal conjugation of the verb *ukan* (*dit, digu* instead of *daut, dauku*. Also cf. *dio*).

---

11. In fact, *ukan* and its noun form *ukaite* do not exist in the Western dialects, in which *izan* and *izaite* mean both 'to be' and 'to have': *izan naiz*, 'I have been', *izan dut*, 'I have had.' *Ukan* (*ükhen* in Zuberoan) only exists in the East.

As far as Zuberoan is concerned, it has undoubtedly borrowed the sound *ü* (*u* in French) from the neighboring Romance language. It has nasal vowels, affricative consonants (but not *v*) and voiced affricatives; *au* is often replaced by *ai* (*gai* instead of *gau*, 'night'). There are many vowel contractions. Voiceless occlusives are rarely pronounced after nasal or liquid sounds (*hánko* cf. *hango*, 'from there'; *gálthe* instead of *galde*, 'to ask'). There is a tonic accent (*áita* cf. *aita*, 'father'). The suffix for the third person plural is *–e* instead of *–te* (*die* cf. *dute*, 'they have.' Also cf. Bizkaian). The genitive possessive is often used instead of the locative to form the future, with participles finishing in the consonant (*kantatüren* cf. *–tuko*). Allocutive forms are used to the maximum. The present potential is used as a synthetic future tense (*dáte*, 'it will be'; *dükégü*, 'we will have it'). The partitive is used in specific synatical contexts.

History of the Language

Forms

The first surviving sentences in Basque are tenth-century annotations discovered in the monastery of San Millán de la Cogolla [La Rioja]: while they are undoubtedly Basque in appearance, their sense is not fully understood.

Rabelais's famous text (*Pantagruel*, IX) was poorly written down and is hardly representative of the Basque of the time. The linguistic form in the first literary works, such as Bernard Etxepare's *Linguae Vasconum Primitiae* (Beginnings of the Basque Language, 1545), is very close to current Basque, the main difference being that the authors of the time frequently used synthetic verbs that are no longer used. For instance, Etxepare writes *eztazagut*, 'I am not familiar with it' (from the verb *ezagun*); Axular writes *badakusazue*, 'if you (plural) see it' (from the verb *ikusi*); Leizarraga writes *dantzuzkigu*, 'we listen to you (plural),' (from the verb *entzun*). Only the latter writer's work includes archaic dated forms that are difficult to understand, using the auxiliaries *di-* and *za-*, along with verb roots, to form the simple past: *etor zedin* cf. *etorri zen*, 'he/she arrived'; *eros zezen* cf. *erosi zuen*, 'he/she bought it.'

Nowadays, while the language continues to lose its richness and resources little by little, and its vocabulary becomes increasingly Latinate—that is to say, "modernized"—it cannot be said to be in danger of dying out any more: it structures are impermeable to any bastardization.

Geographical Area and Use

While it has been stable within its boundaries in the area in France, the Basque-speaking area has continued to contract in Spain. At one time spoken even in areas of Burgos (eleventh century), over the following six centuries the language crept back as far as Pamplona-Iruñea, where is has not been used since the early twentieth century. Now it has been abandoned in the mountains of Navarre as well.

However, in the "loyal" provinces it is subject to an internal dismantlement. The prestige enjoyed by Spanish and French have reduced it to the state of a language that, being of no use, has become harmful: for many years it was preferable to ignore it even for bilingual speakers. The game, however, is not yet lost.

Literature

All literature, in the widest sense of the term, reflects the structure and concerns of the society it comes from. In the case of the Basques, rather than lamenting—as has so often been done—the fact that it has never contributed any works to world literature, it should be taken into account that their great thinkers have always been bilingual, and that writings in Basque have always been aimed, above all, at monolingual Basque speakers. Furthermore, the works of a high standard—except for a few rare exceptions—have been written with moral and religious purposes. Latin, French, and Spanish have been chosen for non-propaganda works because the readers knew those languages as well, not because Basque was not fit to express abstract ideas, as can been seen in the exceptions we have just mentioned.

Folk Literature

There is a considerable body of folk literature of high quality, but it is only known to the extent to which orally transmitted works have been written down and, in many cases, these works have lost their meaning on being removed from the circumstances of their creation. Three types of writing have survived:

In the first place, folk stories. As well as stories that have only been published in translation, there are numerous bilingual collections including, for example, those in the second volume of R. M. Azkue's monumental *Euskalerriaren Yakintza* (The wisdom of the Basque Country); Angel Irigaray's *Euskalerriko Ipuiñak* (Short stories from the Basque Country); J. Barbier's *Légendes du Pays*

Basque (Legends of the Basque Country); Mayi Aritztia's *Amatto-
ren Uzta* (Grandmother's harvest); as well as those published by J.
M. Barandiaran in *Anuario de Eusko-Foklore*, some of which have
also been published under the title *El mundo en la mente popular
vasca* (The world in the minds of the Basques).

These stories usually contain elements of fantasy, often combining mythological beings with characters borrowed from Christian traditions: Jesus or God himself (*Gure Jainkoa, Jinko Jauna*),
frequently accompanied by Saint Peter (*Jondone Petri*), Mary
(*Andre dena Maria*), or the devil. There is no doubt that witches
(*sorginak, beljagileak*) have played a crucial role in this country's
folklore and that the importance of witchcraft, at one time, led to
tragic consequences.

As well as folk stories, proverbs must be mentioned. They were
among the first things to be considered worth writing down and,
as a result, there are very old and extensive collections such as the
anoymous *Refranes y sentencias* (Proverbs and sayings), written
in archaic Bizkaian and published in Pamplona-Iruñea in 1533,
and which have come down to us thanks to a seventeenth-century
manuscript: Zuberoan Arnaud d'Oihenart's collection, published
in 1657 by that very versatile writer (see below).

The last type of writing we will mention in the context of oral
literature are the songs, a folk treasure dearly loved by the Basques,
who are always ready to sing as soon as they get together: at a
party, after a meal, when the wine starts to brighten voices and
loosen them up. As people seldom sing alone, a second voice usually accompanies.

There are innumerable songs and they cover the most varied
subjects: the homeland, the sea, soldiers' misfortunes, love, and
wine, not to mention patriotic and satirical subjects. If we bear in
mind that all folk poetry is first written to be sung, it comes as no
surprise that the lyrics of many of the songs were written by some
of the poets we will mention below. People sing the songs of Etchahun, Iparraguirre, and Elissamburu in the same way they sing *Jeiki
jeiki etxenkoak, Boga boga mariñela, Iruten ari nuzu, Urzo xuria*

errazu, *Maitia nun zira*, *Zantizikitin* and *Kaiku*, whose authors are unknown.

There are numerous collections of songs, such as J. D. J. Salaberry's *Chantes populaires du Pays Basque* (Folk songs from the Basque Country, 1870). And the source remains as productive as ever: current affairs just have to keep up with it!

Bertsolariak (Oral Improvising Poets)

In between traditional folk songs and poetry, which is often anonymous, and a poet's individual work, there is work by a type of singer-poet unique to the Basque Country, the *bertsolari*. They are virtuosos in meter and rhyme who generally make use of their talent in pairs at celebrations held for the purpose, rivaling each other in the quick improvisation of rhyming, sung responses to their partners about the subjects given by the organizers.[1] Some of them have become famous, such as the Zuberoans Etchahun (see below) and his eldest child Beñat Mardo in France. Nowadays, the works of *bertsolariak* are published: tape recorders have made this much easier for editors.

Folk Theater

While it is limited to a single province, and the production there is modest, the originality and reputation of a last folk genre makes it worth mentioning: the Zuberoan *pastoral* theater, undoubtedly a successor to the medieval mystery plays, and the last survivor of

---

1. The pressure that is inherent in this art form leads to improvised juxtapositions of images, which are sometimes unexpected, but which can be wonderful if the *bertsolari* is talented. Here are two examples of this:

> *Mendi gainean, harroka; bide gainean, karrosa;*
> *Etxe huntako etxeko-alabak iduri baitu arrosa.*
> (On top of the mountain, the rock; on the path, the cart;
> The daughter of the house is like a rose.)
> *Itsasoan lanho dago Baionako barraraino;*
> *Nik zu zaitut maiteago xoriak bere umeak baino.*
> (There is mist on the sea up to the reef of Baiona;
> I love you more than a bird its chicks.)

this type of folk theater, which was once popular in neighboring Béarn as well.

The plays are acted in the open and the stage is built on trestles; the decoration is as conventional and basic as the theater techniques themselves. One door represents Paradise, inhabited by angels and "Christians"; the other, Hell, where "satans" and "Turks" rule. In this Manichaean universe, directed by the "pastoral teacher," semi-historical or legendary figures are played by an all-male cast, wearing brightly colored, multi-colored, conventional costumes, with female characters also being played by men.

For five or six hours they confront each other, and recite monologues or dialogues in rhyming verse in a monotonous tone, sometimes accompanied by musical instruments. Subject matter ranges from the Old Testament or pagan times, seen from a medieval perspective, to contemporary history. Naturally, all *pastoralak* [plural spelling—ed.] end with the victory of the "good people" and the discomfort of the "bad people."

The most recent pastoral (1973) was about Antso Azkarra (Antso or Sancho the Strong), the medieval Navarrese count. It was performed in Altzai [Alçay] for the first time and was a success. *Pastoralak* are tragic or, less frequently, comic. It is to be regretted that so few of the scripts have been published (see, above all, G. Hèrelle's works) to an appropriate standard for the purposes of study.

The noisy *asto-lasterrak* (donkey race) plays, which are also Zuberoan, are connected to the *pastoralak*. Their purpose is to punish a member of the local community who has broken the established conventions, particularly in questions of marriage and married life. See below for information about the Zuberoan *maskaradak*.

Individual Literature: Writers

It is difficult to paint a complete picture of this in just a few pages. We are going to quote names and classify them by genre and period, without forgetting issues of dialect, and will limit ourselves, in our comments, to giving brief descriptions of the most important authors.

Epic Beginnings

While anonymous (and, at the end of the day, the *Poema del Mío Cid* and, despite the famous *Turoldus*, our *Chanson de Roland*, are also anonymous), we must mention certain epic fragments quoted by historians such as the *Chanson de Berterretch* (Song of Berterretx), and others that have reached us through popular traditions. They tell us about collective events and bloody wars and rivalries dating from the fourteenth and fifteenth centuries.

To the south of the Pyrenees, we must quote the *Song of Urrejola* (second half of the fourteenth century), the *Song of Pedro de Abendaño* (1443), and the *Burning of Mondragon* (1448). To the north of the Pyrenees, in Zuberoa part of the tragic poem *Chanson de Berterretch* (first half of the fifteenth century), along with its melody, have been preserved by oral tradition.[2] Other ancient fragments, which are more family orientated than epic, are closer to folk literature, which we have already dealt with.

From the sixteenth century to the present, literature has been divided into religious, moral works, and "lay" genres, whether poetry or prose. There are works in genres. There are a remarkable number of works that deal with Basque grammar and defend the language, which is no more than the natural reflex of a people with such a unique treasure and which, farthermore, is so little esteemed by neighboring peoples.

The Sixteenth Century

This period is dominated by three major figures.

---

2. Let us quote two lines, which are also reminiscent of the other works mentioned above:

> *Haltzak eztü bihotzik, ez gaztanberak hezürrik;*
> *Enian uste erraiten ziela aitunen semek gezürrik.*
> 'The plane tree has no heart, nor does cheese have bones;
> I didn't believe that the son of the house told lies.'

Beñat Etxepare, parish priest of Eiheralarre [Saint-Michel], published his *Linguae Vasconum Primitiae* in 1545. It is a short collection of religous and lay poetry (the latter, sometimes, of a highly realistic nature), in which he also sings to the glory of Basque and of being proud to be the first to write in the language (in the Lower Navarrese dialect).

Joanes Leizarraga, from Beskoitze, was also a priest, and published a translation of the New Testament (along with two minor works) in 1571. His work is of great value to linguists because of his deliberate use of archaic forms, which are not all easily understood nowadays.

Lastly, the historian Esteban Garibay Zamalloa, born in Bizkaia in 1533, put together two collections of proverbs. The manuscript of one of them is kept in the Madrid National Library and was not published until the nineteenth century. A similar collection, but anonymous, was published in Pamplona-Iruñea in 1596 and titled *Refranes y sentencias comunes en Bascuence, declarados en Romance* (Common proverbs and sayings in Basque written down in the Romance language); it is written in very archaic language. It cannot be ruled out that Garibay may have been the author of this book, too, and, that being so, all of his work on proverbs has come down to us.

The Seventeenth Century

The outstanding authors are almost all from the provinces to the north of the Pyrenees, and their main subject is moral and religious instruction, which was everything at the time.

The greatest writer was unquestionably the Navarrese Axular, born in Urdazubi [Urdax] in the second half of the century, and was parish priest of Sara. His sole work, *Gero* (Later), was published in 1643 and is a long petition full of Latin quotes, which like many humanist works of the previous century, disparages those who, through weakness, put off the moment for acting or behaving virtuously. His prose, which is Lapurdian Basque with touches of Lower Navarrese, is a model of simplicity, elegance, and fine construction and hardly seems archaic to contemporary readers.

A dozen years earlier (1630) a doctor in theology, Joanes Etxeberri, from Ziburu [Ciboure], had published his *Noelac*, religous poems that do not limit themselves to Christmas issues, as the title might lead one to think. He wrote two more religious works.

It was in Bizkaia, in Bilbao, that Dr. Rafael Micoleta wrote his *Modo breve de aprender la lengua vizcayna* (Short method for learning the language of Bizkaia), which was not published until the nineteenth century. Its linguistic interest is in its marginal character, using an already long bastardized form of speaking.

Silvain Pouvreau, from Bourges, was Duvergier de Haurane's secretary, with whom he learned Basque (the Lapurdian dialect). He became parish priest of Bidarte [Bidart] and published, in Paris, translations into Basque of many educational works. These included *Introduction à la vie dévote de saint François de Sales* (Introduction to Saint Francis of Sales's devoted life) or *Philotea* (1664) and a magnificent French-Basque dictionary.

In 1657, the Zuberoan Arnaud Oihenart, from Maule, published one of the classics in Basque literature in Paris: his collection of 706 proverbs in Lapurdian Basque, with accompanying poems by the author, was a good illustration of both the author and his great work of scholarship (in Latin). His *Notitia utriusque Vasconiae tum Ibericae tum Aquitanicae* (News of the Two Vasconias, both in Iberia and Aquitaine, Paris, 1638), is also invaluable for our understanding of the history of Basque. Another Zuberoan, Jean de Tartas, from Sohüta [Chéraute], parish priest of Arüe, published *Onsa hilceco bidia* (The good way to die) in 1666 and, in 1672, a second religious book. The honor of closing a century in which Basque literature—which until then had been looking for its own style—had come of age fell to the Jesuit priest Bernard Gasteluzar, who published his fine *Eguia Catholicac* (Catholic truths) in 1686.

The Eighteenth Century

During this century literature flourished to the south of the Pyrenees, both in Bizkaia and Gipuzkoa.

The Lapurdian priests Michel Chourio and J. De Haraneder, from Donibane Lohizune, only translated religious works; the only exception was Pierre d'Urte, also from Lapurdi, and who later became a priest, who wrote *Grammaire cantabrique basque* (Basque Cantabrian Grammar) and *Dictionarium Latino-Cantabricum* (Latrin-Cantabrian Dictionary), which has not been published. However, the best work to the north of the Pyrenees was done by Joanes Etxeberri of Sara (1668–1749), a doctor, who wrote a didactic book, *Eskuarazko hastapenak lagin ikhasteko* (Basic Basque for learning Latin), and a book in praise of Basque, *Eskuararen hastapenak* (Basic Basque), a book in which there is as much enthusiasm as there is realism.

The great Gipuzkoan Jesuit Manuel Larramendi (1690–1766), a man of singular character, led the way for other writers of religious and educational books, as well as providing invaluable information for historians, with his *El imposible vencido, arte de la lengua Bascongada* (The impossible conquered, the art of the Basque language, 1729), *Diccionario trilingüe del Castellano, Bascuence y Latin* (Trilingual dictionary of Castilian, Basque, and Latin, 1745) and *Corografía o descripción general de la Muy Noble y Muy Leal Provincia de Guipúzcoa* (Chorography of the very noble and very loyal province of Gipuzkoa, written in Spanish and not published until 1882).

Bizkaian priest Agustin Cardaberaz (1703–1770) wrote *Rhétorique basque* (*Eusqueraren berri onac*; The good news in Basque). Navarrese priest Sebastián Mendiburu (1708–1782) wrote with more style than Cardaberaz. Other writers included the Navarrese Joaquin Lizarraga (1748–1835) and the Gipuzkoan Franciscan Juan Antonio de Ubillos (1707–1789).

"Literary" Basque theater was founded by Father Pedro Ignacio Barrutia, from Bizkaia, whose *Acto para la Noche Buena* (Act for Christmas Eve) is unique in the originality of its ideas and also because it seems to stand apart from everything else written at the time. However, two fellow Bizkaians joined the list of first rate Basque writers at the end of the century. While Pablo Pedro Astarloa (1752–1806), from Durango, only half wins his place in this context with the publication of his works written in Spanish such as *Apología de la lengua vascongada* (Defense of the Basque language, 1803) and *Discursos filosóficos* (Philosophical discourses), which were rationalist in the Age of Enlightenment manner, Juan Antonio Moguel Urquiza [Mogel Urkiza] (1745–1804), born in Eibar, is one of the great names in Basque literature. As well as writing religious works—he was a priest—he wrote the famous book *Peru Abarca*, in which the myth of the noble savage is taken to rural Bizkaia, and in which realism and optimism are combined, making it a good lesson in social morality for the period.

Other Moguels also produced interesting works. The priest Juan José (1781–1844)—the former writer's nephew—wrote works of religious instruction and his sister, Vicenta (1782–1854) wrote prose fables. Many religious prose works were also written, such as those of the Gipuzkoans Juan Bautista Aguirre (1742–1823), José Inazio Guerrico (1740–1824), Francisco Ignacio Lardizábal (1806–1855), the Bizkaian Father Pedro Antonio Añibarro (1748–1830), and, lastly, Father Bartolomé de Santa Teresa (1768–1835), also from Bizkaia and an excellent prose writer and a talented orator.

A special place much be reserved for Gipuzkoan Juan Ignacio Iztueta (1767–1845), who, as well as writing a history of Gipuzkoa—which is not a consistent work—published a remarkable description of the dances of his province. Gipuzkoan Agustin Pascual Ituriaga (1778–1851) wrote fables in verse, which brings us to poetry. It was a northern Basque, the Zuberoan *bertsolari* Pierre Topet, known as Etchahun (1786–1862) from Barkoxe, who shone in this genre. The personal drama that made him famous and obliged him to lead an itinerant existence inspired him to write moving elegies, while he used his often fierce satirical talent to write small masterpieces that are still sung today, along with his elegies, in his native Zuberoa.

The Nineteenth Century

The three most important characteristics of the century were a certain renovation in the northern provinces; the development of lyrical poetry; and the impulse that Prince Louis-Lucien Bonaparte

(1813–1891) gave Basque literature. Nor must we forget the Zuberoan Augustin Chaho [Agosti Xaho] (1810–1853), a "leftist" visionary who wrote extensively and with great imagination about the Basques and the Basque language, although he wrote almost nothing in Basque.

The decisive role played by Napoleon's nephew and the son of Lucien Bonaparte, a passionate researcher into Basque dialectology and linguistics, inspired the work of other writers and translators: Jean Duvoisin (1810–1891), from Ainhoa in Lapurdi, captain in the customs service, translated the Bible and also wrote, among other things, *Laborantzako liburua* (A book about agriculture) in dialogue form; the Zuberoan priest Emmanuel Inchauspé (1815–1902), from Zunharreta [Sunharette] in Zuberoa, was a polygraph and his contribution to linguistics was *Le verbe basque* (The Basque verb, a fundamental piece of work that was published in 1853); the Gipuzkoan Gregorio Arrue (1811–1890), a born translator for all types of writing, and the Bizkaian Franciscan José Antonio Uriarte (1812–1869).

There were some illustrious poets. As well as the Lapurdian priest Jean-Martin Hiribarren (1810–1866), a well-known singer in his home province, the most famous poets were the two Gipuzkoans José María Iparraguirre (1820–1881), author of the hymn *Gernikako arbola* (The tree of Gernika, 1851), who lived the unstable life of an itinerant *bertsolari*, and the romantic, sentimental Indalecio Bizcarrondo, known as Bilintx (1831–1876), whose unhappy life did not stop him from writing both love and satirical poetry. However, it was Jean-Baptiste Elissamburu (1828–1891) of Sara who dominated the period due to the quality and breadth of his poetic inspiration that was both melancholy and Epicurian—though never excessively so—and whose work has been extensively used in folk songs. Another Lapurdian, Gratien Adéma, known as Zaldubi (1828–1907), a priest, also has a place among the poets, although he is less prestigious.

At the end of the century, marked as it was by the disappearance of the *fueros* in 1876, two characters whose work was reminiscent of that of Bonaparte stood out. Jose Manterola (1849–1884), from

Donostia-San Sebastián, published his three-volume *Cancionero Vasco* (Basque songbook) and founded the magazine *Euskalerria* (The Basque Country). Arturo Campión (1854–1936), from Pamplona-Iruñea, is better known as a grammarian and dialectologist than as a writer: the Bizkaian poet Felipe Arrese Beitia (1841–1906) took part in the "floral games" [cultural festivals—ed.] he established.

At the same time, Marcelino Soroa and Toribio Alzaga founded modern Basque theater in their city, Donostia-San Sebastián, and at Ziburu, with works such as *Iriyarena* (1872) and *Anton Kaiku* (1882).

And two priests from Lower Navarre, Jean-Pierre Arbelbide (1841–1905) and Basile Joannateguy (1837–1921) closed the century with their educational works written in clear, elegant prose.

The Twentieth Century

All the authors we are going to mention in this section were born after 1860. With one exception, we will not deal with living authors because our idea of them is not yet set and their work has not yet passed the test of time. There have been talented authors in all genres, more to the south of the Pyrenees than to the north. The first half of the century was dominated by three people whose role was decisive even though there own work was not strictly literary.

First, there was the Bizkaian priest Resurrección María de Azkue (1864–1951), who was the initial director of *Euskaltzaindia* (the Academy of the Basque Language). His work can be divided into two main areas: linguistics (*Diccionario vasco-español-francés*, Basque-Spanish-French Dictionary, 1905–1906); *Morfología vasca* (Basque morphology, 1925; innumerable articles and essays), ethnography (*Cancionero popular vasco* (Basque folk song book, around 1922); *Euskalerriaren Yakintza* and Basque Studies (Basque Studies, in 4 volumes, 1935–1947). He also wrote numerous novels and plays.

Another Bizkaian, Sabino Arana Goiri (1865–1903) combined his resolutely nationalist and home rule oriented political activity with an excessively purist understanding of the language, and this led him to substitute ancient loanwords from Latin and Romance languages—words as old as the first surviving texts in Basque—with daring neologisms, of which almost none have survived. His poetry is of undeniable quality.

Julio Urquijo Ibarra (1871–1950) founded the much missed *Revista Internacional de los Estudios Vascos* (International journal of Basque Studies), which regularly published articles with high scholarly standards. The Bible was exceptionally well translated (*Itun Zar eta Berria*, The Old and New Testament, published as a whole in 1958) by the Jesuit Father Raimundo Olabide (1869–1942). Born in Vitoria-Gasteiz, he had learned Basque at the age of twenty-five in Salamanca of all places.

Abbot Jean Barbier, from Donibane Garazi, wrote mostly folk stories (*Légendes du Pays basque*, 1931). His use of ethnography in the novel *Piarres* (1926–1929) inspired two true storytellers: the Bizkaian Evaristo Bustintza, known as Kirikiño (1899–1929), who wrote *Abarrak* (Little branches), and the Lower Navarrese Enrique Zubiri, konwn as Manezaundi (1867–1942). The Lower Navarrese doctor Jean Etchepare (1877–1935) wrote two collections of essays and memories written in a precise, elegant Basque that made him one of the best prose writers: *Burutxakak* (Ears of corn) and *Beribilez* (By car). The Bizkaian priest Domingo Aguirre (1865–1920) wrote good novels, particularly *Kresala* (Seawater) and, above all, *Garoa* (Fern), written in the Gipuzkoan dialect and which tell the stories of a small port in Bizkaia and a country village in Gipuzkoa respectively.

Having mentioned the highly successful fables (*Alegiak*) written by the Lower Navarrese Jules Moulier, known as Oxobi (1888–1958), we finish this long list with the names of two of the best Basque poets, the Gipuzkoan José María Aguirre, known as Lizardi (1896–1933), who died far too young, and who, in his prose work *Itz-Lauz* (In plain words, 1934) and his collection of lyrical poems *Biotz-begietan* (In the heart and the eyes), proved to be a magician of evocation, intensity, emotion, and poetic depth; and Nicolás Ormaechea [Ormaetxea], known as Orixe, born on the boundary between Navarre and Gipuzkoa, who summarized and synthesized the whole complexity of the Basque soul in works such as his great poem *Euskaldunak* (The Basques, 1950), written in language that is harmonious, simple, and rich at the same time, and whose diverse fresco of folk songs evokes the whole of existence, the seasons, occupations, games, festivities, joys, and sorrows of traditional Basque people.

Part 4

The Basques and Their Economy: Ethnographic Context

In this last section, we are going to try to sketch the context in which the Basques have lived and live today, due to conditions brought about by their geographical situation and by arbitary factors: in other words, the models they have put together collectively. This will lead us, perhaps in extreme cases, to the character of the people: in natural surroundings very similar to those which are so decisive in their neighbors' ways of life, if not identical, they have constructed types of behavior and ways of life that are very seldom similar. On the one hand, material and spiritual modernity have reached them with somewhat of a delay, due to their ethnic isolation and, on the other, they themselves only accepted these changes with a certain reluctance, distrusting anything that could lead them to be identified with other peoples.

Traditional Ways of Life until the Nineteenth-Century Industrial Revolution

People and Surroundings

Communications and Transport

In France, the communication network was rudimentary under the Ancien Régime: in the mid-eighteenth century, there were two fairly bad roads, one connecting the foundries in the Baigorri Valley with Kanbo and the other from Baiona to the Spanish border—the road to Madrid—that went through Donibane Lohizune. Toward the start of the century, two roads were built out of Baiona, one to Puyoo and Pau, the other to Pamplona-Iruñea and passing through Donibane Garazi and, in Spain, Orreaga. And if Basque peasants to the north of the Pyrenees could only go from one village to another on foot or on the back of a mule, it is easy to imagine that the situation was no better in the southern provinces. For transporting merchandise, the passable roads were used by ancient carts with wooden axles and solid wheels that made terrible cracks and holes in the road surface, like the "great groaning chariots" the poet wrote about;[1] the tides, which go between 10 and 20 kilometers inland, made shipping of large loads possible by boat, both upstream and downstream. However, the total amount of freight transported in this way was derisory.

---

1. "Grands chars gémissants": The proverb *Orga txarrago, karranka handiago* ("The worse the cart, the louder the noise") was a reference to this noisiness.

Resources and Techniques

Livestock Farming

This was the fundamental resource for the inhabitants for the Pyrenees.[2] As corn was unknown before it was brought from the Americas, mountain dwellers needed wider and wider areas for livestock
farming, so pasture lands ate away at the forests, and allowing herds
to be driven through culitivated land often caused them harm.

As in all livestock regions, the use of pasture lands was regulated by a wide range of local customs and agreements. Common
lands belonged to the whole village, or to villages grouped together
as valleys or areas. These rights of collective use went beyond
borders;[3] the rules establishing these rights were called "agreements of connection and passage" (*faceries* or *facheries*).[4]

The introduction of corn changed this way of life just as it rev-
olutionized agriculture. It was now possible to feed herds in stables
with this cereal, which led to a considerable increase in livestock,
out of all proportion to the human population. However, corn did
not solve all the problems: herders and farmers carried on disput-
ing land until the nineteenth century, often using violence. The former were determined to maintain their rights of passage while the
latter wanted to increase their returns by expanding their farming
lands and improving production. While there was strict impartial-
ity about this in Spain, in France the farmers were favored, which
led to serious conflicts. In fact, communal lands were very seldom
sold and split up; in the end, herders were only allowed passage

---

2. It seems that the word *abere* (domestic animal) is derived from the Latin *habere*
(to have, possess), and the word *aberats* (rich) is derived from *abere*. In Latin, farthermore, the word *pecunia* (wealth in money) was derived from *pecus* (herd), so they
were the same type of archaic society.

3. Some such agreements are still in force today between French and Spanish
herders, such as that between Gascon herders from the Barétous Valley and herders from the Spanish Basque valley of Erronkari (the "Tribute of the Three Cows"
paid at Pierre-Saint-Martin on June 13 by the Gascons to the people of Erronkari in
exchange for grazing rights in Spanish territory).

4. The existence of these two forms of the word is due to a characteristic of Basque
phonetics.

after the harvest had been collected. This situation, which had stabilized by the eighteenth century, deteriorated once more after the French Revolution and a little later in Spain. The founding of *syndicats pastoraux* (herding lobbies) in France in 1838 brought peace.

Agriculture

This was fairly primitive until the sixteenth century and livestock was the most important type of farming. The need to let the land rest led to leaving it fallow, meaning that it was unproductive for several years. This constraint was remedied by doing *labaki*, a Zuberoan term meaning clearing and weeding communal lands for agricultural use: but this was no last resort and, in some places, was used until the eighteenth century.

With regard to the crops grown in Basque lands, they depended—and still depend—on latitude and climate. In the late twelfth century, cereals, vines, and even olive trees were cultivated to the south of Pamplona-Iruñea. In northern areas, where the climate is cooler and more humid, apples were the most important crop—and they were used to make cider, *sagardo*—while some cereals, above all millet and barley, were grown for local use or for paying taxes (the dough, so to speak). Vines were grown throughout the southern provinces, above all in Gipuzkoa and Bizkaia, for making *txakoli*. The production of this white wine did not diminish until transport was improved.

When maize was introduced (see above), agriculture was transformed and improved considerably. This exotic cereal (which was known as *arto mairu* or 'Moorish maize'; cf. *milh mòro* in Gascon), which adapted perfectly to the climate, particularly in northern areas, became popular and was now simply called *arto*.

It is a crop with many advantages. The land has to be frequently hoed in order to keep it clear and other crops such as beans and pumpkins can be grown between the maize plants, the former plants then rotting and becoming fertiliser for the latter, while the stems, after cutting, can be used as manure. Leaving the land fallow can be replaced by biennial rotation, letting the land regain strength during the winter (or planting turnips for livestock consumption) between harvest time and the time for sowing the maize again (in May). Now better fed thanks to this new cereal, the population started to grow considerably, and the quality of life also improved. This difference was not so marked in southern areas, where maize did not replace the traditional cereals and was a secondary crop.

The continual development of agriculture and livestock farming (for which of maize only served to supplement the use of ancient pasture land) seriously damaged the forests, which had once covered almost the whole land, and whose resources were systematically exploited, as well as being the natural habitat for horses, who lived there in a semi-wild way, just as *pottokak* (Basque ponies) do on the hills of Lapurdi today.[5]

The tools used are striking in their originality: In the first place, the strangeness of the archaic, heavy, difficult to use, and inefficient *laia* has led to it being interpreted (by Th. Lefebvre) as a clumsy European adaptation of a lighter tool used in the Americas for growing maize, and imported along with that cereal.[6]

Animal-drawn tools include, first, the old *golde-nabar* (*golde* meaning swing plough, from the Latin *culter*, to grow; *nabar*, ploughshare), which was carved on many disk-shaped gravestones, and whose large, separate ploughshare is drawn on a harness parallel to the rest of the plough, which makes working it easier. The plough (*golde* or *perja*, from the Gascon *pèrja*) was made of wood, and later or iron, and was different from the model used in neighboring

---

5. This destruction of the forests, being replaced by grazing land or heathland (with gorse and heather, which livestock can make use of), has led to some strange terminology on French maps: the woods of Senpere, Hazparne, and Amikuze are described as heathland: the name remains although the reality has changed.

6. With regard to light tools, some writers see the Occitan *bigós*, a type of two-pronged hoe, as the etymological heir of a supposed Basque two-pronged instrument, *bi-(h)ortz* (two teeth). However, the word *bigós* is not Gascon, and S. Palay only includes the form *bigót* is his *Dictionnaire du béarnais et du gascon modernes* (Dictionary of modern Béarnais and Gascon), definining it as a two-pronged hoe. The question remains open.

areas, being rectangular in shape and that, according to some writers, was introduced by the Suebi, a Germanic tribe.

With regard to vehicles (cf. the abovementioned "groaning carts"), full wheels were used throughout the Basque Country until recently, and are still used in Spain, while in the northern provinces an original type of cart (*orga*) has been adopted, with its platform resting on a Y-shaped beam ending in a slat-sided wooden construction with a type of windshield fixed to a vertical bar coming from the beam.

Fishing and Hunting

There are plentiful salmonidae, salmon, and trout in the rivers and streams of the country. The former, which, in the egg-laying season swim up the Aturri, Errobi, and Ühaitza, is extensively fished; the latter have always been fished from streams in the Pyrenees. Sea fishing was, originally, an essential food resource for the coastal population.

While there had always been fishing with nets along the coast, it was the Vikings (Normans), who raided the Basque coast between the ninth and eleventh centuries (in 892 they decapitated Saint Léon, the first bishop of Baiona), who introduced harpoon fishing.

From then onward, the Basques did not limit themselves to fish, hunting the small whales (*Balaena biscayensis*) that were then numerous in the Bay of Biscay, with lookouts on watchtowers built on high points along the coast using smoke signals when a whale was spotted. When that species began to become rare, from the seventeenth century onward, they started hunting bowhead whales (*Balaena mysticetus*), which they had to go much farther for, sailing by the British Isles across the North Atlantic to the Artic Ocean near Newfoundland and Canada. Competition from England and Holland, both maritime nations, dealt the Basques whale hunters a fatal blow and, during the second half of the seventeenth century, they stopped hunting. They had discovered cod in Newfoundland, and they went there to fish it until the nineteenth century.

Basques on the Spanish coast had also long fished sardines, which are abundant to the west of the Bidasoa. After 1750, this example was followed along the French coast, above all in the nineteenth century; the fish caught was sold in Donibane Lohizune to lively *Cascarotes* (Bohemians) who, barefoot and with their baskets on their heads, hurried to Baiona to sell their merchandise.

With regard to hunting, the most valued game is the pigeon (*urzo, uso*), mostly shot when migrating over the moutains, through the well-known "passages" in Sara, Etxalar [Echalar], Aldude [Les Aldudes], and the Oxkixe [Osquich] Pass, in closely formed groups. There, the camouflaged lookouts and beaters in the trees or on high towers on poles throw sparrowhawk-like baits into the air, in this way bringing the pigeons down to narrow passes in which they are caught in the giant nets thrown over them.

Small-scale Industry and Crafts

From being herders and farmers, the Basques took from these two main activities of theirs the primary materials for certain rudimentary, almost craft-like industries. For instance, leather was used in the many tanneries and shoemakers, while clog makers used wood from Pyrenean oaks and which, in fact, also provided dye. With regard to textiles, sheep provided wool (in many places in Gipuzkoa and in Hazparne *marraga*—sack cloth—was made; cf. the Gascon *marrègas*).[7] Thick wool, linen, was produced in humid northern areas, spun and woven by each family, which would then use it itself.

Among these local activities, some are not so "classic" or widespread in craft terms (seamstress, blacksmith, wheelwright, carpinter, mason, and so on); some are more specific, such as makers of *kaiku* (typical wooden recipients, with a slanted profile, which were used mainly for carrying milk and boiling it by putting hot stones into them); *ferreta* (the Gascon *herrada*), round buckets made of wooden slats with metal hoops (which are what give it

7. From the pre-Latin root *marr-/mard-, 'goat, ram,' cf. the Gascon *marrèga, 'old ewe.'

its names, although they were generally copper), wider at the bottom than at the top; *xahako*, a small wineskin of Navarrese origin; and *makila* (from the Latin *bacillum*), a medlar wood club with leather throngs and copper nails, which was made as a considerable weapon during the nineteenth century by adding a hidden punch on the handle, the best-known maker of these sticks being based in Larresoro [Larressore] (Lapurdi).

We will look at craftsmen farther in the context of the house, customs, and games.

Mines and Foundries

Basque land is relatively rich in coal and minerals, but coal can only be mined extensively in the Bilbao area, from where it is easily exported by sea. Lignite from Gipuzkoa and Navarre is obtained in very modest quantities. However, there are considerable metal deposits, iron being the most important production in the country.

Compared to copper, lead, and zinc, which, perhaps except for copper, are of minor importance in industry and of which there are insignificant deposits, iron is exploited wherever there are mineral deposits of it. But metal work led to forges being set up in wooded areas and wood—or charcoal, which, at the end of the day, is the same—was the sole source of fuel; forges were near flowing water in order to temper the metal. The sources of wood, the sale of which benefited local communities, were not renewed so quickly, and the distance from which fuel had to be brought led to the forges closing down being, as they were, the hungrier for fuel the more they prospered. For instance, the Banka copper forge in the Baigorri Valley was only open for two centuries (1555–1767); the iron foundary outlived it but was open for even less, ceasing to function in 1786. They used very primitive techniques.

Bizkaian iron and coal, on the other hand, played, and continues to play, an essential part in the country's economy. Exploited since the tenth century, the excellent minerals were worked, in the nineteenth century, with pinewood charcoal from Les Landes, at the Aturri River foundries.

Trade and Smuggling

As both the road network and means of land transport were rudimentary, Basque trade was mostly carried out using sea transport.

To the north of the Bidasoa, the strength and stability of trade led to changes in the riverbed of the Aturri. Until the twelfth century, it joined the sea, as it does today, at Baiona, a city that was founded due to its special position (*Lapurdum* has existed since the Gallo-Roman period, cf. Lapurdi – *Labourd*, in French). The silting up of the river mouth made it necessary to look for another way out to the sea, farther to the north at Capbreton which, favored by this circumstance, became a rival to Baiona. However, during the first half of the fourteenth century, Capbreton also became silted up and a way out to the sea still farther north was chosen, at Vieux-Boucau, which seemed to menace Baiona for good.

In order to defend its own interests, Baiona built a seawall in 1578 that put the river back into its original course. However, the river silted up again during the following century, and a fourth way out to the sea was found at Biarritz, which was also favored by its proximity to Donibane Lohizune (this was the great period of Louis XIV's marriage there).

Finally, in 1729 Baiona was given permission to dredge the Aturri and channel it out between the new seawalls, which Napoleon had extended as far as the sea. However, sea currents are unstoppable, and the reef, which is still there, would always hinder Baiona's economic development.

The small ports all along the coast between Baiona and Bilbao traded foodstuffs, indispensable to the coastal population, using the sea up to the early nineteenth century. This trade was classified as "reciprical treatment" (*traités de bonne correspondance*) and the Franco-Spanish wars never put a stop to it, coastal navigation carrying on uninterruptedly.

With regard to large-scale, transatlantic trade, this enabled the Spaniards to export their products to Northwest Europe, England, and Flanders. The Basque ports were well positioned to be bases or ports of call for freight ships. After the conquest of America, these ports declined as Cádiz profited, being the starting point for expeditions to the New World.

When customs barriers led to the Spaniards stopping importing from Northwest Europe, they started importing goods from the Americas, which Donostia-San Sebastián became an entrepôt and distribution center (the Compañía Guipuzcoana de Caracas had the monopoly of this trade).

During the sixteenth and seventeenth centuries Baiona, which was ideally situated geographically, was also a commercial port for trade with Spain. Its prosperity declined during the following century, at the same time as Bilbao's iron, on the other hand, made it easy to foresee that the Bizkaian port was going to grow from being a merely local port.

Smuggling, a natural consequence of the customs taxes imposed between France and Spain, was not only a considerable source of income for people in border areas (we are not dealing here with just "small-scale" smuggling, which, while producing benefits for those involved, does not seriously harm the two neighboring countries' economies). It also fitted in with two constant atavistic factors in Basque character: refusal to recognize boundaries that arbitrarily separate two halves of an ethnic whole, and refusal to blindly accept authority, above all when it is not autocthonous.

Basque Society

Human Groups and Customs, Family and Neighbors, Habitat, and Local Areas

Traditional Basque society, which is essentially rural, seems to have always been very stable, closely connected to solid family structures, and, in a wider context, probably by the fact that individual and collective liberties have been considerably reduced by crises such as that which affected France in 1789.

Family and Neighbors

The family was the basic social unit everywhere until the nineteenth century and still remains so in many places, symbolized by the *house*.

Usually several generations live under the same roof: the master and lady of the house; the parents of one of them (to whom they have passed on the inheritance) who, having become subordinate, sometimes find themselves in an unfavorable situation; and the younger couple's children. To this add one or two servants and, often, a brother or sister of the heirs, having remained unmarried and accepted to help keep up the house.

For it is the law of primogeniture, or birthright, which has long ruled Basque society: wisely preserving the estate (split up, it would no longer be profitable), which the eldest descendant, son or daughter, would inherit (unless, that is, the parents named somebody else).

This meant that their brothers and sisters, who were often numerous, had to go elsewhere to find their place in society. While the girls were naturally destined to form a home in another house, the boys could emigrate and try to make their fortune "in the Americas," go into religion, into a seminary, or even join the army, unless they became craftsmen in their own villages.

The constraints implicit in such an economic and social structure explain, to an extent, the care with which parents planned and prepared the heir's marriage, whether boy or girl. Love matches were, perhaps, the exception. On the other hand, there was equality between the master and lady of the house in terms of their responsibilities at home, both in material terms (having the same workloads) and moral terms (girls as well as boys being able to inherit). We should point out that equality is still a fundamental law in Basque society.

The house that the inheritance was based around had a name and, in the Middle Ages, this often became the family's name, and the house's name is still more important than the family's: it is unchanging, whereas when a female heir marries her surname changes.[8] It is this attachment to heriditary property that is reflected in the Spanish Basque custom of adding the suffix –*tar* to patronymics, in this way stating where they live.

Female heirs are good matches (see the song "Prima eijerra," The Beutiful heiress). In times of difficulty, families would receive invaluable help from first neighbors (*auzoak*), for example when doing hard work such as turning over the land (*laia*), when a family member was ill or had died, for instance. The status of first neighbor involved honorific and agreeable compensations (taking part in family festivities, for example, or easy access to basic supplies), and could involve regular obligations such as *lorra* (obligation) in Bizkaia. The ability to find help like this is particularly appreciated in such wide areas of low population density.

Habitat

This is closely connected to the different physical conditions in different regions. In mountain valleys, people tend to come together in hamlets (barrios) and in villages (each proprietor also having his/her farm in the hills). On the plains, urban areas are also built at the most favorable economic sites: on riversides or at main river mouths, at ancient crossroads, and so forth.

However, most of the Basque Country is hilly, and agriculture is usually based around farms, generally built on slopes,[9] so villages, in themselves, are usually no more than a few houses around the church, the cemetry around it, the village hall, the school (if there is one), and the *pelota* court.

It is this white farmhouse on the hill, surrounded by livestock and crops, which traditionalist writers and poets have feted and presented as the idyllic, peaceful setting of life in the Basque Country (see Elissamburu's famous song "Ikusten duzu goizean," You

---

8. This is true throughout the Western Pyrenees, still being the case as far as Comminges and Couserans and in Béarn.

9. The possibility cannot be excluded that this topography protected the Basque ethnic group from the harmful effect of invasions dating from Antiquity up to the Middle Ages that often destroyed or assimilated local populations.

see it in the morning). This is, indeed, the reflection of a reality, even if existence has not always been as easy and serene as has sometimes been made out.

In some areas, such as in Zuberoa, the farms are grouped together in hamlets that, in turn, come together to form municipal areas. Mitikile-Larrori-Mendibile [Moncayolle-Larrory-Mendibieu], with its three centers, has no more than 400 inhabitants; Larzabale-Arroze-Zibitze [Larceveau-Arros-Cibits], in Lower Navarre, has no more than 500.

Local Areas

While contour designs the natural valleys, it is the Basque hills that sketch the geographical areas, of varying size, in which people live and in which, as in the mountain valleys, they have their own characteristics. While the various ancient tribes gave each individual "province" its original individuality, in its turn each natural area has developed a type of collective awareness with which its inhabitants relate, marking them as different from their neighbors. This fact, simple as it is, has seldom been made use of by ethnographers and linguists, who should find the key to the existence of the truly different dialects there.

These local areas are more ethnographic than strictly geographic units, and can be defined in terms of particular types of behavior and use of language. We have already mentioned the boundaries of the Baigorri local area (which is, in fact, a valley) and of Uharte-Garazi, Arberoa, Oztibarre, and Amikuze. As well as the areas that are valleys in themselves such as Erronkari, Aezkoa, and Baztan (cf. the Aran Valley, which is now Gascon-speaking and has its own definite character), there are other local areas such as Bortzhiriak (Cinco Villas, The five towns) and Burunda. These areas have often been used in determining political boundaries and they are very much alive in peoples' consciousness.

Customs and Beliefs: Religion, Myths, Rites, and Witchcraft

Among the Basques, as throughout the rural populations of Christian Europe, traces of ancient pagan beliefs and archaic mentalities have been conserved to an extent, combined, with varying degrees of success, with the new religion and with rational types of thought. Perhaps the long survival of paganism among the Basques and their relative ethnic isolation have helped them to maintain these beliefs.

Religion, Myths, and Rites

There is almost no direct information about the Basques' original religion. Only Aymeric Picaud, in his pligrim's guide to Santiago de Compostela (the *Codex Calixtinus*) mentions "*Deum vocant Urcia*" (A god called Urcia). It is possible that this name, which, in the form of *ortzia*, meaning "the sky" in Erronkari Basque, is connected to the modern terms *ortziri* (thunder), *ortzegun* (Thursday) (cf. *Donnestag* in German – literally, "Thunder Day"), and *ortzirale* (Friday), and was used to describe any divine atmospheric event. It would seem that Zeus and Jupiter had a similar origin, if one is to believe their etymology! However, there were many other particular figures in the Basque pantheon of gods, if one is to judge by contemporary myths.

The ethnographer J. M. Barandiaran made exaustive research into the legends and myths of his country (*Anuarios de Eusko-Folklore*; Basque Folklore Annuals) and found an impressive list of gods (while it is true that there may have been specific deities in each region). We will underline the snake *Herensuge*, known almost everywhere; the terrifying *Tartalo*, a sort of cave-dwelling Cyclops; his reassuring counterpoint *Basa-Jaun* (Wild Lord), who, accompanied by *Basa-Andere* (Wild Lady), protected the harvests and herds; and, above all, the female figure *Mari*, a powerful spirit with hundreds of attributes, whose subterranean dwellingplace is linked to all the caves and chasms in the Basque Country; and the "Condemned Hunter" (also known as King Solomon), who crosses the sky with his pack of hounds on winter nights: *Salomon Errege* or *Eiztari Beltz* (the black hunter).

At a more humble level, there are the *Laminak*,[10] small feminine spirits who haunt the fields, and who sometimes help local people using their magical power or sometimes play tricks on them, a little like French *fées*, or, even more, like the Gascon *hadas* and the Catalan *encantades*.

In the context of Christianity, which has been so firmly implanted in the Basque Country (in Roman Catholic form), it should be remembered that "God" is called *Jainkoa* or *Jinkoa* (literally, 'the God'), and, formerly, *Jauniko*, which seems to be an oscure term reinterpreted and "corrected" as *Jaun-goikoa*, 'the Lord on High.' The "Devil," who, according to Oihenart (seventeenth century), the Zuberoans used to call *Tusuri*, is nowadays known as *debru* or *deabru*, a Latin term, like all terms connected with religion: *eliza* (church), *gurutze* (cross), *apez* (friar or priest), *aingeru* (angel), *arima* (soul), and so on.

With regard to family rites (which some would call superstitions), these are present in all the important moments of rural life. Their regional diversity and variety of form defy all description. We should underline that, nowadays, they are often to be found in Christianized forms, being carried out on traditional religious holidays. But, then again, the same can be said of Saint John's Day (Midsummer Night's Eve), and of Carnaval, accompanied though they are by Christian symbols: the cross, sprinkling of holy water, candles, and so forth. Most of these rites are also known throughout the valleys in the Pyrenees.

The relatively late introduction of Christianity into the Basque Country (no earlier than the tenth century), must have led to a sort of "reversal of mythical values," which can be clearly seen in two places: In one case, a Roman votive altar to the local deity Aherbelst has been found at Comminges. If one takes the name to be Basque, it easily becomes *aker beltz* (black ram), the central character that witches are supposed to meet around at the *akelarreak* (covens). In a "positive" Aquitaine Basque pantheon of that

---

10. Perhaps descendents of the Roman *Lamies*.

period, surely that figure would have been grouped in the "negative" world of the demons.

In another case, Basque legends often talk about the *Jentilak* (cf. the Gentiles), in other words, the pagans who populated the world before Christianity: they are bizarre, worrying types of men, disagreeable to deal with, and, in some cases, believed to be buried under dolmens.

There, too, the prestige which had formerly been attributed to the Romano-Gauls, the possesors of power and civilization, had given way to contempt mixed with fear.

Is it not moving to see, almost two thousand years later, the living memory of such a decisive moment in Western history still firmly fixed in the collective memory?

Witchcraft

So it is no surprise that wizards and, above all, witches (*sorginak; belhagileak* in Zuberoa) have played an important role in Basque society. There are innumerable legends about them (see *akelarre* below), and belief in their curses is still widespread.

It is important to know that at the beginning of the seventeenth century the most spectacular witch trails were held in the Basque Country under the supervision of Pierre de Lancre, member of the Bordeaux Parliament, during which, as part of a long period of collective hysteria, hundreds of presumed wizards and witches were condemned and burned after pleading guilty.

Material Surrounding: Houses, Popular Art, and Dress

Houses

Their economic and social role, as well as real and symbolic importance, deserve greater attention than that which we can give them here. In fact, while the different type of houses in the territories are, naturally, connected to their geographical situations, the structure and characteristics of the basic type of house—whether in Lapurdi, Lower Navarre, Gipuzkoa, and, to an extent, Upper Navarre and Bizkaia—are highly original.

It is a half-timbered stone or brick building (or made of both materials) with a tiled roof whose top (*bizkarra*) is perpendicular to the east-facing façade. On the ground floor there is a canopy (*ezkaratz*) that is as important as a room in itself and that is used for sorting crops and storing vehicles. It is also in this central area (which leads to a backroom), on the first floor, that the kitchen and bedrooms are to be found; immediately above, the attic is lit by triangular skylights and, in some cases, gives onto a wooden gallery in which crops are dried. The central block is prolonged on one side or on both, generally asymetrically, by the stables, above which there may be more bedrooms.

In the central and western parts of the country the *ezkaratz* is open, and the façade above the ground floor is open half-timber, with the wood of a dark color—usually reddish brown—and the wall bright white in fine contrast.[11] In Lower Navarre and Spanish Navarre, on the other hand, the *ezkaratz* is closed by a curved doorway, with the frame and arch are carved in large slabs of pink sandstone, as are the window frames, the smallest ones facing west and the half-timber there hidden.

This type of construction can be easily understood as deriving from a type of construction built on piles that left the ground floor open for storing vehicles, with the first floor being inhabited; this also explains the wooden framework remaining visible. The lateral stables are a later addition that create the assymetry of the ground-plan and the façade.

There are also many isolated granaries built on piles, following a pattern much more common farther west, for example in Galicia. This architectural model—which, in the latter case, protects crops from harmful animals—may well be a descendant of the prehistorical stilt house: another ancient trait that contributes to the Basque countryside's originality and that is also a real aesthetic success.

---

11. The aesthetic qualities of these façades have led to them being copied by architects in the building of thousands of ornamental villas. The "Basque style," whose very pronounced characteristics often match poorly with other local styles, has been all the rage outside the Basque Country.

Popular Art

Many types of simply made objects are decorated and, in that decoration, there are a certain number of ornamental themes.

Inside the house, furniture such as cupboards, chests (*kutxak*), and high-backed benches (*züzülüak*) are to be found in Zuberoan halls; chimney plates or chimneys themselves. Outside, it is often doorplace lintels, which are very richly decorated in Lower Navarre, on which decorative themes are accompanied by inscriptions "signing" and dating the house; or the upper part of *pelota* courts. In cemeteries, too, in which disk-shaped gravestones[12] are typical on Basque graves (and which can be see throughout the very west of Europe), as well as the Lower Navarrese black and white tomb crosses.

These ornamental themes are varied: five-pointed stars; fan or spiral-shaped motifs; commas that, grouped four by four, make up the "Basque cross," very much like a swastika, and also well-known in other forms of popular Basque art. Drawings of objects, tools, or religious things are not unusual, being added as an epigraph to certain letters: the capital A, for instance, has a horizontal line similar to a T, and this the way is used to specify which is which on ocasion.

In conclusion, two original features in French Basque religious architecture: In Lapurdi and Lower Navarre, many nave side walls hold two or three wooden galleries, nowadays reserved for men.[13] In Zuberoa, there were generally three gables of unequal length (the middle one being the longest) at the end of the clock-gables, sometimes known as "Trinitaries" or "Calvaries" (this form changes slighly in the north of the province and crosses over into Béarn).

---

12. The interpretation of this object is unclear: does it represent the sun? A stylized head? This is not known.

13. It is believed that this arrangement was a response to an exceptional growth in population during the Ancien Régime.

Dress

The only ancient dress we will deal with is that mentioned by Aymeric Picaud, who compares it to the Scots costume: a sort of tunic that ended at the knees and rough leather sandals called *lavarcas* (*abarkak*[14] are still used today in different forms, but are increasingly being replaced by espadrilles—*espartinak*—with hemp soles) tied onto the foot. To this, on occasion, was added a black woolen hood with fringes that went down to the elbow (*saia*), which seems to have lived on in the form of the *kapusai* on the other side of the mountains.

Before the beret (*bonet* or *ponet*, *gapelu* or *xapel*) became popular (which was not before the seventeenth century, and which later became part of the Carlist uniform[15]), Basque men wore long rimmed hats and Basque women wore a type of horned turban, which some have seen as a phallic symbol, until the seventeenth century. Young girls, who wore their hair close-cut, went bare-headed. Head scarfs (*burukoak*) nowadays only cover a bun, if one is worn.

For a long time the mountain people of Navarre wore short trousers and stockings, which were common in the French Basque Country until the Revolution and in the Spanish part of the country until the War of Independence [the Peninsular War—ed.].

In daily life, for a long time Basque men wore a long woolen belt, the *gerrikoa* (cf. the Catalan and Occitan *cinta*) and a pleated black shirt, the *xamarra*, which was replaced, on feast days, by the *maripulisa*, a short red, woolen jacket. Still today, Basque women are glad to wear huge black mantles—*kaputxak*—in church or at funerals. But the most spectacular costumes come out, nowadays, at folk festivals and other such ocasions.

---

14. Perhaps, in very ancient times, they were made from bark, which could mean that the word was derived from *abar* (branch).

15. The *Requeté* red beret is still worn in Navarre.

Festivities, Music, Dances, and Games

Festivities

Perhaps those at the start of the year are the livliest: carnaval, when the *maskaradak* are held, above all in Zuberoa.

Two groups of boys in costumes are formed. The first is the red *maskarada*, made up of *Txerrero* and his horse hair broomwhip and, formerly, the "lambs" and the "bears"; *Gathüzain*, the "cat," with his extendible scissors; *Kantiniersa*, a man dressed as a woman auxiliary soldier; *Zamalzain*, one of the main characters, wearing a turban, holding the reins of a pretend wicker horse that he makes rock backward and forward using the bridle (which is where his name, meaning "horse rider" comes from);[16] the *Kükül-leroak*, dancers dressed like *Gathüzain*; the *Marixalakak* (blacksmith farriers); *Enseinari* (lieutenant), with his flag; *Jauna* and *Anderea* (the master and the lady); *Laboraria* and *Etxeko-anderea* (the farm worker and the lady of the house); and, finally, the musicians. The characters in the black *maskarada* are humbler, and the list may vary to an extent: gypsies, coppersmiths, odd-job men, a doctor, a pharmacist, and so on, as well as a black *Txerrero* or *Zamalzain*.

The groups march and pretend to fight with spectators who get in their way; each character in turn carries out a series of mime dances; they symbolically attack the village, which has put up a barricade defended by the *Basa-andere* (Wild Woman). Then there are dances, little scenes in which each characters plays its costume's role (including the *Zamalzain*'s *godalet-dantza*, 'glass dance'), and, to conclude, a ball.

One hesitates to speculate about the origins and meaning of *maskaradak*, which do seem to resemble old pagan rites.

After the May Festivities, in which a May Queen (*maiatzeko erregina*) is chosen, the festivities are not so exceptional. The most important ones are the Saint John's Day (Midsummer Night's Eve) or solstice festivities, whose pre-Christian origins are well-known:

---

16. This is the "horse-petticoat" or *chivau-frus* in French and Provence folklore.

the worship of the sun, water, and vegetables. At night, a wood fire is lit, and people jump over it to cure themselves and defend themselves from all sorts of evil and curses; the houses are decorated with hawthorn, poplar, and ash branches; with the same aim in mind, water from certain fountains is drunk; people wash themselves with dew and swim in streams.

The saint's festivities, generally celebrated in summer or fall (and, formerly, at the same time as certain major fairs or markets) must, originally, have been harvest festivals, celebrating the crops, richness, agricultural abundance. The collective dance was the main merrymaking on this ocasion (see below).

The year finishes with Christmas (*Eguberri*, New Day) and *Olentzero*,[17] of unknown meaning, and New Year's Eve (*Gabon*, Good Night), when a traditional yule log is burned: its embers are believed to have apotropaic properties and must be kept half-burned to be used again on stormy days, when they are placed in the hall as talismans.

Music

First, the instruments. There are three types of three-holed wooden flute (all with two holes on the front, one at the back). The *txistu* measures 42.2 cm [approximately 16.5 inches]; the *txirula* (the French Basque *txistu*), 32 cm [approximately 12.5 inches]; and the *silbote*, made up of two parts which fit together, 61.8 cm [approximately 24 inches].

The *ttun-ttun* or *soinu*, the French Basque tambourine,[18] which is carried on a strap when played, is struck with a stick using the right hand while a *txistu* is played with the left hand; it is a wooden sound board of a long, trapezium shape (90 cm [approximately 35 inches]) in whose underside there are two orifices; there are six

---

17. This is also the name of a grotesque and brutal mythical character who is said to come down the chimney to warm himself at the Christmas fire. In fact, this type of announcer of Christ is the Christianized avatar of a pagan winter solstice god, of whom there are other examples in other European countries (according to J. Caro Baroja).

18. This is also used in neighboring Béarn (*tamborin*).

strings that go along it and that are tuned using keys; instead of striking the *ttun-ttun*, a *txistulari* can use a small drum in the same way (*danbore, danboliñ*), which is taller than it is wide, while a tambourine player can also play a flat drum (*atabal*) using two sticks.

These types of instruments, the most typical, are documented from the sixteenth century onward. There are other, less usual ones: the Bizkaian *alboka*, which is made of two unequally sized horns connected by pierced reeds; the Basque drum, *pandero*, which is connected to the use of bells and cowbells in music.

With regard to folk melodies played with these instruments or sung, they are mostly highly rhythmic and fast. 5/8 time, which is extremely rare elsewhere, is very common.[19] The unknown origins of many popular melodies are later revealed to be no other than lay versions of religious tunes: this explains the common contrast between the lively, satirical lyrics and the innocent-sounding music, seemingly monotonous, over which people sing!

Dances

Voltaire called the Basques "that small nation that sings and dances at the foot of the Pyrenees." And, in fact, dancing comes as naturally to the Basques as singing does and there is dancing—in groups, as in all folk dancing—for every occasion.

Saint's day balls start with the *aurresku* or *gizon-dantza* (the men's dance), a solemn, "official" dance. It is followed by the *gazte-dantza* (the young people's dance); *etxekandere-dantza* (the ladies of the house's dance); *mutil-dantza* and its French version, the *mutxiko* (the young people's/servants' dance). Some dances bear the names of the parts of the body they use: *esku-dantza* (hand dance); *bizar-dantza* (beard dance); and *ipurdi-dantza* (bottom

---

19. Except, perhaps, in the Balkans, for instance in Greece – if we limit ourselves to European music. This peculiarity is certainly due to an essential characteristic of Basque music, and which has been adopted as a symbol of Basque music: Iparraguirre's hymn *Gernika* is 5/8, and Maurice Ravel, who was born in Ziburu, either due to love of his homeland or musical whim, used it in *Quatuour, Danse général* in *Daphnis et Chloé*, and so on.

dance). Others take the names of the characters they are about or what those characters do: *sorgin-dantza* (witch dance); *zapatain-dantza* (shoemakers' dance).

When there is group dancing in the streets (*edate-dantza*, 'drinks dance'; *karrika dantza*, 'street dance'), the stages of processions come to mind: *katadera-dantza* (hunting dance); the dangerous *almute-dantza* (grain measure dance); *godalet-dantza* (glass dance). And, finally, the very moving *ezpata-dantza* (sword dance), which begins with the dancers kneeling down to salute the local flag or the Basque fleet by bowing their heads; they end by acting out a fight that concludes when the stiff "corpse" of the captain is borne off horizontally by the group.

Closely connected to dancing are the Basque "jumps" (*jauziak*), whose name is confusing with regard to their real nature. They are choreographies for men in which only the feet are used, and so used with great agility, using twenty or so established patterns. Local groups compete in terms of presentation and agility.

Games

The most famous game is undoubtedly *pelota* (*pilota*), which is a descendant of Jeu de Paum (the palm game), which was well-known under the Ancien Régime. The oldest versions are direct games in which the court is divided into two halves, as in tennis, and the wall is of only secondary importance. Part of these games was the rebound, which was regulated by complicated laws involving a specific version with a buffer, as well as the version known as *pasaka* (with leather gloves), which was seldom played.

Indirect games, known as *pleka*, were first played in the early nineteenth century and involved the ball bouncing off a wall or *frontoia/fronton* before being hit again by the player. This was played in the open air or in covered halls (*trinkete/trinquet*). One player hit the ball (*pilota*) with his naked hand (*esku huts*), or with a wooden raquet (*pala*), or even with a leather glove or—better still—a long, curved wicker basket called a *xistera* fixed to the wrist, using a technique invented around 1857.

The rhythm of the game depends on how the ball is served. It is fast when played with the naked hand, with *palak* and with "small gloves": this is *joko garbia* (a clean game). However, when played using large gloves the game is slower, making up in strength and nobility what it looses in liveliness, volleys becoming harder to keep up, and, often the ball can hit the ground before being hit back. The rules are complex and cannot be explained here.

There are other games that also involve skill and strength, but they are nowhere near as renowned as *pelota* and are mostly played to the south of the Pyrenees. An original game called *palanka* involves throwing a ball (*palanka*), in the manner of darts and discus and following various patterns. There are axe competitions (*aizkolari*) that involve cutting a pile of thick beech tree trunks as quickly as possible. There are weight-lifters (*jasotzaleak*) and stone-piercers (*harri-zulatzaleak*). Lastly, we should mention the very popular card game *mus*, played using the Spanish deck.

Cuisine

Generally spicy, inspiration often comes from Spanish cusine (olive oil!) and habits from Béarn and Les Landes. The best known recipes include: On the coast, fish soup or *ttoro*; Bizkaian *bakailua* (dried cod in tomato, onion, garlic, and almond sauce); *marmitako*, a tuna stew with peppers and tomatoes. In all areas, *eltzekaria* (also known a *salda* or *kozina*), a traditional stew or soup made using pulses; "Basque chicken," seasoned with peppers; the famous *piparrada* (also known as *biperra ta tomatia*), a sort of omelet with the ingredients added in highly variable proportions; and, if possible, ham! Local baking mostly involves a family cake known as *pastiza*, as well as the justly renowned Donibane Lohizune macaroons. Wine from the Irulegi hills is, perhaps, mistakenly overlooked in favor of *Izarra* liqueur, which is yellow or green and made of mountain flowers. Lastly, Baiona's specialty, chocolate, must be mentioned.

Basques outside the Basque Country

Traditional social structures and the preocupation with protecting exploitable property have led younger sons, right up until the present day, to seek their place outside the family inheritance. Many left home in that way and, until recently, were still leading the rough life of herders or workers "in the Americas" (*Ameriketan*), in North America (California, Nevada) and South America. Some of these Basques (known at home as *Amerikanoak*, 'the Americans') have stayed there, but most have returned to their home towns or nearby after making their fortunes.

In former times, this need to emigrate was combined with a taste for maritime adventure,[20] and this led to many Basques becoming famous as explorers, from the fourteenth century off Greenland (Newfoundland, also known as the Isle des Basques or "Island of the Basques") when hunting whales, to the sixteenth century: Juan de la Cosa, Elcano, Legazpi, and Urdaneta led Basque crews to discover the New World, where Irala, Garay, Ursua, Aguirre, Recalde, Ibarra, and the Oquendo, Lezo, Mazarreda, and Churruca families conquered land, while saint Francis Xavier evangelized Asia. Other Basque names are to be found in the annals of European intellectual discovery, names such as Jean de Sponde [Joanes Ezponda] and Duvergier de Hauranne.[21]

The *Amerikanoak* who emigrated for good have sometimes managed to reach the highest places in their respective new societies, certainly if one looks at the names of many heads of state in South America.

---

20. See pp. 39–40 for information about Basque privateers; the southern provinces produced just as many.

21. See p. 81.

After the Nineteenth-Century Industrial Revolution

While the rhythm and way of life had changed very little in the Basque Country since the sixteenth or seventeenth century, the disappearance of old structures was accompanied with the advent, in the nineteenth century, of techniques and economic models connected to mechanization.

Communications and Transport

While, at first, roads were less developed than the railroad network (from 1864 on, the railroad from Paris to Madrid stopped at Hendaia, Donostia-San Sebastián, Altsasu, and Vitoria-Gasteiz), at the beginning of the twentieth century Bizkaia, and then Gipuzkoa, were the provinces with the most kilometers of roads suitable for motor vehicles. Farther to the east, the mountains hindered road construction, which did not take place in the Zaraitzu [Salazar] and Erronkari Valleys until 1899. The building of railroads away from the coast went slowly for the same reasons of lack of practicality.

Nowadays, roads surpass the railroads: Nationale 10, in France, is being replaced by Motorway 63 (1976), which, coming from Bordeaux, reaches Behobia via Tarnos, and will be taken as far as Donostia-San Sebastián, Bilbao, and Vitoria-Gasteiz. The route along the N 132 and 618, D 20, and Spanish N 121 connects Baiona and Pamplona-Iruñea, passing through Kanbo, Ainhoa, Dantxaria, the Otsondo (or Amaiur [Maya]) Pass, Elizondo (Baztan), and the Belate Pass, is going to be turned into a freeway by building a tunnel under the latter. A second freeway (A15), which is very recent, links Behobia and Bilbao, while a third, which will connect Baiona and Pamplona-Iruñea, will then continue on to Zaragoza. Among other roads planned in France, there is one from Baiona to Atharratze and Hazparne.

There are four airports of medium size near the coast that handle a considerable volume of passengers, merchandise, and mail. These, from largest to smallest, are Biarritz-La Négresse (2,250 m. runway), Bilbao (2,000), Pamplona-Iruñea (1,700), and Donostia-San Sebastián-Hondarribia, whose current 1,600 m. runway is going to be lengthened to 2,100 m.

There are three ports, distributed in the same way as the three main air bases, although differently in terms of their economic importance: first, Bilbao, the port for Bizkaia's industrial area, handling 3,597,700 tons in 1925, 5,754,890 in 1961, and 12,800,000 in 1971; Pasaia [Pasajes] comes far behind, handling 1,850,000 tons in 1961 and 3,749,000 ten years later (350,000 tons before 1914!); Baiona follows closely, handling 600,000 tons in 1925, 1,730,000 in 1961, and 2,785,000 in 1970. We will look at the type of cargo they deal with below.

Livestock Farming

This was an essential resource in the land of the pre- and protohistorical Pyrenean herds.

In high areas, goats, which are too voracious, have been removed from the northern mountain range, except to the west, where their numbers have doubled in ten years: between 1962 and 1971, their numbers increased by 81.8% in Gipuzkoa and 118.2% in Bizkaia. To the south, however, they provide the milk that cows cannot due to the lack of pasture land.

Horses, whose breeding has diminished to the west of Irun, still live wild in the central area of the country, and semi-wild in the southwest, which is colder; they are systematically bred on the northern planes. Mules are bred in mountain areas and fattened for sale in lower areas.

Ovine livestock, the primitive, black-headed *manex* breed from Bizkaia to Lower Navarre and the *ardi xuri* (white sheep) in Zuberoa, which had increased until around 1900, then faced severe competition from bovine livestock, which was bred for urban consumption (in France, the manufacture of Roquefort cheese means that more ewes are bred).

In the valleys, the traditional livestock is still pigs that, in this land of oaks and beeches, are fed at no charge and, when young, they wander around in small groups eating acorns and beechnuts (in mountain areas, deforestation is a serious threat to this); they are fattened, however, on farms.

Bovine livestock has increased considerably to the north of the mountains since the early nineteenth century due to the development of urban life, for which meat, milk, and butter are essential. Between 1812 and 1921, quantities multiplied by five in some places and even by ten in Pasaia. The hardy Pyrenean race is prevalent in the mountains, but there is cross-breeding and mixing on the plains. Herdsmen's lives, along with that of their herds, are still very traditional and archaic, still using collective appropriation customs inherited from the old herdsmen's associations (and which, in 1838, became *syndicats pastoraux* in France; cf. the aforementioned customs in Erronkari) that regulate the way pasture land is used. In the same way, the rights of passage through villages, particularly in mountain areas, is a lasting reflection of ancient customs. Lately, droving has become less important—there are fewer herdsmen and animals are easily fed on farms—but it is still carried out.

Agriculture

In mountainous areas such as Navarre, cultivated areas are being taken over[1] by pasture land, which is basically because infrastructures allow grain produced elsewhere, on the banks of the Ebro, to

---

1. On the plain, the damage caused by phylloxera has reduced vine growing considerably.

be easily supplied, and because the old herding tradition is perfectly suited to the geographical conditions.

On the French side, urban needs have also favored livestock farming, with livestock reducing vine growing and wine being easily procured from elsewhere.

Nevertheless, modern techniques have only slowly been introduced. Around 1930, swivel ploughs were only beginning to replace traditional ploughs on the plains and in the valleys (though it must be said that the latter is probably better suited to mountain agriculture). The same may be said of the combine harvesters, which faced tough competition from sickles and scythes; threshing machines did not do away with cereal crop beating in *ezkaratz* in the north, nor with *trilla* in the south, the latter involving pointed sledges being pulled over strips of land by harnessed animals.

Two archaic practices are worth mentioning. In southern Zuberoa, the distribution of certain pieces of alluvial land among farmers, each one being given a piece of land (*elgea*) in addition to his own land, involved the compulsory alternate sowing of wheat and maize. To the south of the Pyrenees, common land was still cleared periodically (rotations, cf. *labaki*, p. 90) to improve yield.

Fishing

The invention of steam and motor boats, in places where the geographical structure was compatible (not in the ports of Deba and Baiona, for instance, which were too silted up), transformed fishermen's living conditions and led to an enormous increase in production: motors made ships independent of the wind, currents, and inclement conditions.

The only restriction is connected with the type of fish. In spring, there are plentiful anchovies and sardines, although the latter move toward Bizkaia in the summer and toward the Aturri in the fall. The real summer fish are tuna and skipjack; the latter can still be found off the Spanish coast in the fall, where hake, lobsters, and squid are also caught; in winter, there are still sardines, but sea bream is the main catch.

The tons caught has varied by species since the start of the century: in 1962 French Basque fishermen caught half the anchovies they had in 1938, while the catch of tuna had multiplied by six over the same period. The biggest problem, however, is that of overproduction. Efforts were made to solve the problem by developing fish conservation techniques: tinning, transporting fish in refrigeration wagons, and freezing at high sea on ships especially equipped to do so.

Fishing is infinitely more important on the coasts of Gipuzkoa and Bizkaia than it is on the Lapurdi coast. The tonnage landed at Pasaia in 1960 and 1961, for instance, was ten times that unloaded at Donibane Lohizune! At present, French fishing is subject to the EEC and fierce competition from other maritime nations.

Industry

It is, of course, in this area that the most spectacular progress has been made. Ancient sources of energy have been added to hydro-electric energy, which is plentiful in the mountainous northeast, the first station being built at Donostia-San Sebastián in 1886.

First, small industries were set up, modernized, and mechanized: Industries connected to forested areas (clogs and baskets in Gipuzkoa; wooden tool and wicker furniture in Zumarraga; tannin-dyed leather in Hazparne); industries that also used water transport (timber floating and furniture in Gipuzkoa and Bizkaia); industries requiring considerable energy supply (paper in Tolosa); textiles, whose craft production ceased at the start of the century; berets in Gipuzkoa; ceramics in Zumarraga; salt in Mugerre [Mouguerre] and Beskoitze; stone in Bidaxune [Bidache] and Ahurti [Urt].

Heavy industry, mostly metals, was founded in Bizkaia—and, to a lesser extent, in Gipuzkoa—and it became the most important industrial region in Spain. Altos Hornos de Vizcaya, established in 1902, employed 10,000 workers in 1924 and 15,000 in 1967. The high concentration of heavy industry in Bizkaia did not prevent numerous factories being set up throughout the country, as can be seen in Gipuzkoa, except, perhaps, for the Deba Valley, for which an industrial plan has been drawn up. The other provincial capitals are also making progress.

Trade

Infrastructure developments and, above all, the growth of industry brought with them a spectacular increase in trade.

To illustrate this, we will just mention the volume of shipments in the three main ports since the mid-nineteenth century (our statistics are not complete).

In Bilbao, shipments went from 300,000 tons in 1870 to 1,340,000 in 1878, 4,460,000 in 1890 and around 5,750,000 in 1900, falling back to 3,500,000 in 1922, a figure that was nearly achieved again in 1970, with statistics foreseeing growth to 4,400,000 by 1975. The rapid growth was due to industrialization; the following decrease to coal deposits running out, civil and world-wide conflicts; a new strength in recent times. Pasaia, likewise, started with 350,000 tons before 1914 and surpassed this figure—after a decrease during the difficult years—in 1962 (545,000 tons), and tripling it in 1970 (1,500,000 in 1975). The port of Baiona, Le Boucau, which handled no more than 6,380 tons in 1826, grew at an incredible rate over the century, handling 216,000 tons in 1882, 1,025,000 tons in 1913 and, after World War I, 878,000 tons in 1929; after World War II, it recovered and reached the figure of 709,000 in 1962 and 2,785,000 in 1970!

Trade's sound bill of health is also to be seen in the role played by the banks. Two Bizkaian banks are of the first rank: the Banco de Bilbao was founded in 1857 and the Banco de Vizcaya, more recently, in 1901: they are among the five largest banks in Spain. The distribution of trade profits is quite a different matter, and we will not address it here.

Basque Society[2]

Like the political and social structures on which it is based, Basque society has been profoundly transformed, not without friction, and continues to undergo deep changes, although these do vary considerably from one area to another, depending also on the type of surroundings—urban or rural, with all their nuances—and even on the influence that modern tourism has on local populations.

In fact, what we are seeing seems to be a twofold attack on the old structures, even if this is sometimes involuntary. On the one hand, the internal influence of "progressive" factors within society itself—progressive in the widest sense of the term—as opposed to bourgeois, traditionalist, and "reactionary" elements. On the other hand, the influence of factors that have come from outside fortuitously, whose presence, pacific and benevolent as it is—at least in the northern provinces—has, nevertheless, caused a malaise that seriously underminds the "Basque" nature of the society it has come into contact with.

The former factors are the consequences of inevitable social and political evolution. The delicate balance of the old social edifice has been weakened by too many factors: if some young people have questioned and continue to question tradition, sometimes knocking over the most stable conservative strongholds in favor of the "left," the issue is, independently of political ideals, that rural farms are less and less profitable, even for the chosen heirs; the younger siblings are less and less prepared to accept the eldest child's special treatment, which means that they lose out, at the same time as local resources are considerably underemployed due to a policy of easy tourism that gives the country no more than an appearance of prosperity with rural life becoming, even for the heirs, no more than a stop-gap—with too much work and too few sources of entertainment—if they have been able to enjoy urban

---

2. This section is mostly about the "French" part of the country and is largely based on the work of a young sociologist who is involved with studying his native Baigorri Valley: Pierre Bidart.

environments, however briefly, and compare their lot with those of the tourists who visit the Basque Country.

The latter factors are the second "wave of attack," and combine with the "foreigners" established in the country long-term such as civil servants, trades people, or business people. Tourists, who come from Paris (above all) or other places, bring money with them that they are happy to pay out in exchange for displays of folklore, excursions, or regional cuisine (which is done well here), but there is also a negative side to the coin: since people have started behaving *like* Basques on a theatrical stage, for spectators avid to see the picturesque, instead of *being* Basque with their fellow countrymen, local civilization has become commercial folklore, motivations have changed, and all infringements on authentic tradition are permitted because what one is doing is providing *pleasure* to people who are ready to pay (and not all the spectators are informed ethnologists!).

The use of the Basque language in these circumstances is also affected by a similar ambiguity: as it is something that tourists see as local color, it is sprinkled on programs, advertisements, and labels (accompanied by a translation, if possible), but young Basques who have spoken the language from childhood will maintain that they do not understand a single word of the language for fear of being seen as rural or of lesser value next to city dwellers.

In fact, as this contact only lasts for one season of the year, and one finds oneself truly at home once more as soon as the fall reddens the ferns on the hillsides, the damage is not irreperable. The same is not true when the "foreigner" becomes a temporary immigrant (in summer campsites for vacationing families, for instance) or a permanent one: if they become owners of a second home and pay their taxes, they believe that they have the right to demand, for example, a similar degree of comfort to that which they enjoyed in the city, a degree of comfort that, despite progress in the surroundings and housing, the modest level of local income cannot offer without stopping financing other things of vital importance. Even temporary immigrants, in brand new vacation facilities right next to a town, behave in accordance with a type of urban lifestyle that is diametrically opposed to Basque traditions and in which, for instance, neighbors are not devoted, fraternal friends, but rather rivals from whom one wants to differentiate oneself and whom one wishes to surpass in originality and luxury.

Will the pessimistic outlook that these examples illustrate long remain so? Fortunately, that now seems unlikely. Obvious examples of the "de-Basquification" of the Basque Country are progressively being overtaken by other, more encouraging signs: there is a strong return to local values that young people praise once again, basing their outlook on very "current" political options, often in solidarity and communion with autonomist thought on the other side of the Pyrenees. In contrst to "folklore for cash," regional culture is once more in favor with the new generations: thanks to private initiative, Basque is once more taught to children at the *ikastolak* (Basque schools). While Basque culture has long been linked with a certain archaic way of thinking and behaving, and while it is true that previously it was still possible to identify Basque society with a traditionalist point of view, there was not necessarily a cause-effect relationship there. As long as the authorities renounce the use of violence, which can only lead to more violence, and as long as the Basque Country is given economic and social policies that meet its needs, a new Basque Country can be built today, not on the debris of a renounced past but rather based on what was good in the old structures. And, as being Basque is, first and foremost, speaking Basque, may linguists be allow to wish fervently, and for the whole country:

> *Bizi dadin euskara, orain eta beti!*
> May Basque live, now and forever!

Short Bibliography

General Works

F. Michel, *Le pays basque*, Paris, 1857; P. Veyrin, *Les Basques*, Arthaud, 5th edition; G. Viers, *Le Pays basque*, Privat, 1975; E. Goyheneche, *Notre terre basque*, Bayonne, 1961.

Geography

T. Lefebvre, *Les modes de vie dans les Pyrénées atlantiques orientales*, Paris, 1933; G. Viers, *Pays basques français et Barétous*, Toulouse, 1960; C. Dendaletche, *Guide du naturaliste dans las Pyrénées-Occidentales*, Neuchâtel, 1973; articles by P. Lamare.

History

For works on prehistory and protohistory, see publications by J. M. Barandiaran, J. Blot (*Bulletin du Musée basque*) and *Problemas de la prehistoria y de la etnología vascas*, Pamplona, 1966; also see M. García Venero, *Historia del nacionalismo vasco*, Madrid, 1968; M. Ugalde has recently published *Síntesis de la historia del País vasco*, 1974.

Linguistics and Literature

See the works of the Spanish experts R. M. Azkue, A. Campion, A. Tovar, P. Irizar, K. Mitxelena; and the French experts G. Lacombe, P. Lhande, H. Gavel, J. Larrasket, R. Lafon, P. Lafitte, G. N'Diaye; the German experts H. Schuchardt and C. Bouda. See the works of K. Mitxelena, L. Villasante O.F.M., and J. Haritxelhar about literature.

Ethnography and Related Subjects

In addition to the general works mentioned about, see articles by R. M. Azkue (*Euskalerriaren Yakintza*, I-II-III-IV, Madrid, 1942 sqq), J. Caro Baroja (*Los Vascos*, Madrid, 1958), J. Vinson, L. Colas, J. M. Barandiaran.

Journals

We should underline the no longer published *Revue international des Etudes basques* (Paris-San Sebastián, 1907-1936); *Eusko-Jakintza* (Baiona, 1947-1957); *Euskera* (Bilbao); *Gure Herria* (Baiona); *Boletín de la Real Sociedad Vascongada de los Amigos del País* (San Sebastián) and its literary and artistic supplement *Egan*; *Bulletin du Musée basque* (Baiona); *Príncipe de Viana* (history) and, more recently, *Fontes Linguae Vasconium* (linguistics), as well as *Cuadernos de etnología y etnografía de Navarra*, published in Iruñea-Pamplona.

Journals

In France, the weekly *Herria* (Baiona).
In Spain, *Zeruko Argia* (weekly, Donostia-San Sebastián) and *Anaitasuna* (Bilbao).

Index

www.ingramcontent.com/pod-product-compliance
Lightning Source LLC
Chambersburg PA
CBHW020613270326
41927CB00005B/321